Praise for *Conversations for Change*

"A must-read for anyone in business, government, or academia. The lessons she teaches are all too often taken for granted. This work distills a lifetime of experience into easily understood actions that can benefit us all."

—Joseph Major, Chairman and CEO,
The Victory Bank

"Is the conversation you are having with your coworkers, boss, team members, and even yourself meaningful? If not, then it is time to change the conversation. This is just the book to give you the tools to create more meaningful conversations."

—Clark Handy, Senior Vice President,
Global Human Resources, Convergys Corporation

"Having clarity about conversations is especially helpful for an introvert like me who has difficulties thinking on my feet in social situations. With these strategies I have a tool to lead conversations in purposeful directions and not get flustered and frustrated."

—Rod Hanby, Oracle

"Shawn Kent Hayashi has taken the key approach to communication, 'the conversation,' to a level where one can plan out a strategy to be heard, be effective, and enhance the overall communication experience. I enjoyed reading through each of the 12 conversations to determine which ones I was not using because I was not convinced I would be successful. I now have the structure to practice ahead of a real interaction so I can engage with confidence and in a meaningful way."

—Robyn Helmer-Tallon, Vice President–
Talent Management, Peabody Energy

"Communication is one of the most critical skills we utilize in everything we do, personally and professionally. We often take for granted the many different kinds of communications we have with people and as a result don't plan well for success in each of these conversations. Shawn's book is a great practical guide to help us all be more successful in every interaction we have. You will find a chapter that will take you step by step through the critical elements for every conversation to develop a great plan to achieve your goal. This is a must-read."

—Dave Desch, Vice President, IMS Health

"Shawn Kent Hayashi has captured the essence of successful relationships in this blockbuster book. If you have a personal or work relationship that's not working, there's a chapter in this book that will specifically address what to do and what to say to change the conversation to a successful outcome! With sound principles and compelling stories, this book will be a classic for years to come!"

—Elizabeth Jeffries, author, *The Heart of Leadership:*
How to Inspire, Encourage and Motivate People to Follow You

"Creating meaningful conversations is essential for leadership today. As a global leader, you need to leverage all 12 types of conversation to properly engage, motivate, and build a high-performance team. Today, it is likely your team is well educated, globally connected, and ambitious—pulling this high-talented yet diverse group together around a common mission while supporting their individual professional goals takes strong communication skills. Being able to conduct the 12 conversations in *Conversations for Change: 12 Ways to Say It Right When It Matters Most* will help you become a more effective leader."

—Jim Rogers, Market Vice President, Deltek

"Shawn Kent Hayashi takes effective communication and makes it approachable, executable, and successful in this easy-to-read book."

—Gary B. Cohen, author of *Just Ask Leadership—*
Why Great Managers Always Ask the Right Questions

"Shawn expertly analyzes a fact of life we take for granted—"the conversation"—and transforms its meaning and power into an action plan that gets results. Take the plunge and apply her techniques and witness your rapid results from your conversations."

—Laura Fredricks, JD, LLC, author of *The ASK: How to Ask for*
Support for Your Nonprofit Cause, Creative Project, or Business Venture

Conversations
for
Change

Conversations
for
Change

*12 Ways to
Say It Right
When It Matters
Most*

SHAWN KENT HAYASHI

New York Chicago San Francisco Lisbon London Madrid Mexico City
Milan New Delhi San Juan Seoul Singapore Sydney Toronto

The McGraw·Hill Companies

2 3 4 5 6 7 8 9 0   QFR/QFR   1 5 4 3 2 1 0

ISBN 978-0-07-174528-4
MHID 0-07-174528-9

The term *When the Conversation Changes* is a trademark of Shawn Kent Hayashi and may not be used without written permission.

McGraw-Hill books are available at special quantity discounts to use as premiums and sales promotions or for use in corporate training programs. To contact a representative, please e-mail us at bulksales@mcgraw-hill.com.

This book is printed on acid-free paper.

Contents

CONTENTS

Acknowledgments

This book would not have been written without Deborah Callahan's assistance. For two years she was my trusted, faithful assistant. Her High Steady communication style kept me grounded and focused on the next step. I am deeply grateful for the opportunity to work with her. I wish her well now that she has relocated with her family to another state and we do not see each other as often.

Alison Proffit has taken over Deborah's day-to-day role as my assistant, and I am grateful for all the ways in which she supports me in my work and life. Thank you for leading, following, and tugging at me, Alison!

There are so many people to thank for their help, support, kindness, friendship, and forgiveness along my path. Izzy Justice, Bill Bonnstetter, Judy Suiter, Kristy Tan, Jeff Davidson, and Cynthia Kyriazis—thank you for all the ways in which you create conversations to lead and teach me. If we've worked together in any way, I am thankful for your contribution. I look forward to our next conversation.

I am deeply grateful for all my clients who have enabled me to do the work I love so much. Thank you for your trust. I am honored to have the opportunity to work with you. Because I agreed to keep our work anonymous, I'm not listing your names here, but please know I appreciate each of you.

Elizabeth Jeffries, Marilyn Muchnick, Laya Charlestein, Linda Bishop, Toni Moore, Doreen Lechler, and Michele Dayoub, you have been the best friends anyone could ever wish for! I cherish our ongoing conversations.

To my agent, Bob Diforio, and the team at McGraw-Hill, I thank you for your persistence to get it right. Judith McCarthy, Joseph Berkowitz, Janice Race, Staci Shands, and Heather Cooper, I look forward to working with you on many more projects.

Thank you to my family for all you do to support and love me. Jim Hayashi, William Hagan, and Silvia Muscas, thank you for being part of my everyday! I love and adore you!

Introduction

Why do we need to change our conversations?

Sometimes the old way of doing something no longer works. Other times we do not agree with what is happening, and so we need to change direction. Each of these situations requires us to create a new dialogue that will present new possibilities for ourselves and others. Whether we want to create more meaningful relationships in our professional lives or we have to end a relationship that isn't working, these changes are made through our conversations.

As an executive coach, I specialize in helping clients to communicate clearly and effectively in order to build meaningful working relationships through communication and to achieve their goals. I am honored to be able to hear the details of their interpersonal challenges and successes. The validated assessment tools I use as the first step in coaching enable me to see the preferred communication style, workplace motivators, natural talents, and emotional intelligence competencies of each person or team I am working with. All these factors are important because they affect conversations, and conversations enable relationships and organizations to grow.

Sometimes conversations need to change in response to a change that is out of your hands. You hear that a new department manager will be overseeing your group, that your company will be merging with a competitor, or that your team members want more time and attention. Other times you want to initiate a change. Maybe you decide you want to take on a larger responsibility at work with the intention of being promoted. This move will require a conversation in order for your boss to change his or her thinking about your abilities. Perhaps you want to work flextime hours, and you don't think your boss is going to like the idea; or your spouse has been offered a job in another state, and you want to convince your company to let you keep your job and live 500 miles away. These situations require a change in conversation as well.

What causes a conversation to be meaningful to one person and not to another? How can you assess what is meaningful to a person you want to connect with? The answers will become clear as you explore the chapters in this book. You will also come to understand how emotional intelligence, workplace motivators, and each person's preferred communication style impact every conversation you engage in. In these pages you'll have the opportunity to meet some of my clients and read about some of my own experiences working with influencers at all levels of various organizations. In some cases, I have changed the name of the person for trust and confidentiality purposes.

There are 12 types of conversation that are important for growth and success for leaders, managers, and teams. When you are comfortable creating each of these conversations, you will experience confidence and credibility in your leadership style. When one or some of these conversations are missing from your dialogue with others in certain situations, you may not be able to create the success you are looking for. By using the full range of conversations, you can reach your maximum potential for success. To do this though, sometimes you need to change the conversation.

Mamma Mia is an inspiring musical that pulls together seemingly unrelated songs. Similarly, this book pulls together the seemingly unrelated models, ideas, and advice I've used in my work as a coach, mentor, manager, and leader over the past 20 years. The most meaningful conversations are the ones that initiate beneficial change, and this book highlights what worked and what did not work for my clients and me when creating meaningful conversations.

Like any song you enjoy listening to, you will encounter ideas you have heard before as well as new ideas. My hope is that this book will inspire you to review the conversations, models, ideas, and advice that are shaping who you are today so you can create what you really want—so the music you are making flows deliberately and masterfully to create the experiences you want to have. May meaningful dialogue surround you in all your professional relationships.

Our work and the world are both changing so quickly that we need to be able to create conversations that acknowledge the impact of these changes. Your next significant change is about to begin . . . NOW, as you use these conversations in your work.

Conversations
for
Change

PART I

FOUNDATIONS FOR EVERY CONVERSATION

CHAPTER 1

Emotional Intelligence

The first time I heard the term *emotionally illiterate*, I stopped what I was doing. I knew immediately that *I* was emotionally illiterate. Not only did I not have enough awareness of other people's emotions, but I also did not make distinctions around my own. This impacted my ability to build rapport with others in ways I could not understand at the time. I thought about what the word *literate* meant: recognizing words and knowing what they mean, then being able to read words strung together in phrases and sentences. It takes people years to learn how to read words well enough to enjoy reading. Similar to the process of learning to read, learning to be emotionally literate takes practice too. I was motivated to practice because I wanted to be a good communicator.

Having the emotional intelligence to deal with our own emotions first gives us the confidence and ability to navigate through the changes that are inevitable in our careers. We can experience an emotional hijack as a result of a change, or we can self-regulate and catch ourselves before we head into an emotional uproar. We can be aware of how other people's emotions are impacting their ability to have a meaningful conversation. When we know how to process ourselves and others through our emotions, we will be able to create more meaningful conversations. We will be able to create conversations for change.

Once I understood the power of emotional intelligence, it became clear to me that people who are really great communicators are emotionally literate. The difference between star performers and average performers is emotional intelligence. Great communicators connect on every level with their audience in ways that inspire, motivate, and engage others.

The Seven Core Emotions

According to Mike Bradshaw in *Using Emotional Intelligence at Work*, people who are emotionally literate earn more money, adapt better, complete tasks faster, and have fewer career derailments. It became powerfully clear to me that emotional intelligence is foundational to good communication and management. Dr. Izzy Justice, one of my mentors and a highly acclaimed expert in global management, shared with me that seven core emotions show up chemically in the body:

1. Love
2. Joy
3. Hope
4. Sadness
5. Envy
6. Anger
7. Fear

This understanding changed my emotional awareness. To be emotionally intelligent you need to know which of the seven emotions is currently operating in you at any given moment, and then you need to know how to intentionally use that to inform your actions. It's helpful to have a map to guide your direction. Some cars have a Global Positioning System (GPS) that enables you to know where you are at any time. Think about these seven emotions as an interactive "emotional guidance system" that shows you the map of emotions so you can identify where you are now and where you would like to be. You can employ the seven basic emotions as an Emotional GPS.

Each emotion has triggers. For instance, I often feel hope when I begin working with a new coaching client. What triggers you to feel each of the seven core emotions?

1. Love
2. Joy
3. Hope
4. Sadness
5. Envy
6. Anger
7. Fear

Each emotion also has symptoms that show up in our thinking and our bodies. When some people have to give a presentation to a large group, it's often a trigger to feel fear. The symptoms of fear may be foggy thinking, sweaty palms, a shaky voice, or red blotches all over one's face and chest. Each person's emotional triggers and symptoms are unique. In other words, we each have our own customized emotional map.

Emotional Symptoms

Your emotions map is unique to you. Can you map each of these to one of the seven core emotions? Each of these physical symptoms links to an emotion or several emotions:

1. Tapping fingers on the desk as someone speaks
2. Speaking quickly
3. Heart beating faster
4. Giggling
5. Giggling uncontrollably at an inappropriate time
6. Voice becoming loud or high pitched
7. Crying

8. Laughing
9. Sweaty palms
10. Trembling
11. Stomachache
12. Headache
13. Rolling eyes
14. Smiling and singing a playful song
15. Walking with a skip in your step—a little lighter than normal

You will be more emotionally aware when you are able to see the connection between the symptoms and what you are doing now. Ask yourself, "What feeling is underlying my current actions?" This is a way to become aware. Self-awareness is the first step in emotional intelligence. We cannot self-regulate if we are not aware of what we are feeling. When we are aware of what we are feeling, we can also begin to speak about it in a way that builds rapport and empathy in conversations with others.

Emotional States of Being

We are always feeling something. Our emotions are always on whether we are aware of them or not. Ask yourself, "What am I feeling now?" and then pay attention to what is going on in your body, thoughts, and senses. Doing so will help raise your awareness. Each of the following states of being is distinctly tied to one of the seven core emotions. See if you can figure out which ones go together for you:

1. Freedom
2. Passion
3. Enthusiasm
4. Positive expectations
5. Optimism
6. Contentment
7. Boredom
8. Pessimism

9. Frustration
10. A sense of being overwhelmed
11. Disappointment
12. Doubt
13. Worry
14. Blame
15. Discouragement
16. Bitterness
17. Vengefulness
18. Hatred
19. Jealousy
20. Insecurity
21. Guilt
22. Unworthiness
23. Grief
24. Depression
25. Powerlessness
26. Inability to concentrate

Each of us has our own unique emotions map. You are beginning to understand your own emotions map by making these connections. The more you understand what triggers an emotion and how it is expressed in your behavior, the higher your awareness will be, and the result will be that you are able to develop more meaningful communication and connections with others.

Emotional Intelligence Competencies

Being emotionally intelligent involves being self-aware and able to regulate your thoughts and actions so that you deliberately move toward the feelings that you want to experience. Your mission is to consciously conjure the thoughts and take actions that trigger a positive feeling, so you'll be better equipped for communicating with others. By developing these five emotional intelligence competencies you will do just that:

1. *Self-awareness.* Knowing what you are feeling in the moment

2. *Self-regulation.* Deciding what you want to do with an emotion—in other words, being proactive rather than reactive to an emotion—and intentionally shifting your emotional state so that you are not hijacked into behaving in a way you will regret later

3. *Motivation.* Knowing what excites you and playing to your own passions as you make decisions; using your favorite skills and abilities so you enjoy your work

4. *Empathy.* Being able to identify what someone else is feeling in the moment and work that into the conversation to create rapport

5. *Social skills.* Being able to work with a group, to align the group members around common goals to create forward progress

It is important to start with a focus on the first competency—developing self-awareness—because if we are not aware of what we are feeling in the moment, then we are not able to do the other four. If we experience an emotional hijack, it can be devastating to a conversation. With self-awareness we can change our inner conversation about what we are feeling and create different outcomes in conversations with others. To create conversations for change we must be able to process ourselves and others through emotions.

The Emotional Ladder

According to Izzy Justice, "In the sequence of an experience emotions come first. Emotions are faster than thoughts. That means emotion trumps competencies, behavior, and character unless we learn to be self-aware and channel our emotions consciously." Next time you are in a public place where you can observe people, perhaps on a subway or at a conference, see if you are able to identify what emotion another person is experiencing just by looking at that person. When you have practiced this, you will be able to look at people and get a sense of which emotion they are currently marinating in.

Many people are stuck emotionally and do not even realize it. I know professionals who are stuck in sadness, anger, or fear and dread going into their offices. One of my clients describes her high-rise office building as the "tower of doom." She describes the people who work on the floor she does as "sad worker bees." Although she was very optimistic when she started her new job six months ago, as she has gotten to know her peers and management, she realizes most of them are emotionally stuck and do not know how to process themselves through their emotions. Change is unlikely when we are stuck.

If we want to create strong professional connections with others, we need to create an emotional connection with ourselves first. Once you are aware of your own emotional triggers and symptoms, you can move up the emotion ladder. Think of the seven core emotions, repeated here from above, as an emotional ladder:

1. Love
2. Joy
3. Hope
4. Envy
5. Sadness
6. Anger
7. Fear

When we are stuck emotionally, we stay in one emotion for a long period of time. We carry that emotion with us into the next thing we do. It is as if we have an emotional set point, and the emotional thermostat keeps us in the same emotional temperature. A conversation can change this. I refer to this as processing ourselves through an emotion.

Have you noticed when a conversation changed your emotional state? Perhaps during a job interview in which you discovered that the position was a wonderful fit for your abilities, you noticed yourself shifting to excitement (joy); or alternatively if you realized the position was not a good fit, you may have experienced sadness. You could be carried by that emotion for a long while, taking that emotion into everything you do the rest of the day. Or you could intentionally choose another feeling if you are aware and able to self-regulate.

To move up the emotional ladder, you have to stop judging your own emotions. This is a key to getting unstuck emotionally, too. You can stop oscillating in a stuck emotion by being aware. Ask yourself, "What am I feeling this moment?" Acknowledge the feeling, breathe into it, and notice what arises.

When we feel anger, we need to acknowledge that feeling. Anger is a signal that something has crossed our boundaries. The emotion is begging for a conversation to deal with whatever or whoever crossed our boundaries. Whenever you feel stuck in anger, ask yourself, "What's going on that I need to have a conversation to clean up?" Create that conversation. Are you self-aware enough so that the next time you notice anger, you will ask yourself, "What crossed my boundaries, and whom do I need to talk to in order to clean it up?"

Then, focus on the next highest feeling, and proceed up the ladder of emotions. Think the thoughts and take the actions that you would if you were feeling joyful, and soon you will be. Try this without judging yourself, and you will experience amazing results.

Intentionally think thoughts and take actions that enable you to choose the next highest feeling on the scale and make decisions from higher emotional states. The conversations outlined in this book help a great deal in cleaning up issues, problems, and conflicts so that you can continue to move up the emotional ladder.

Shifting from a Problem Focus to a Solution Focus

Emotional intelligence is not hardwired. It can be developed at any age. It takes consistent and focused practice to become emotionally intelligent. People who learn from their experiences have significantly higher emotional intelligence than those who do not recover. When we do not recover, we get stuck in that emotional pattern and re-create it again and again. We talk about it too much and do not move on.

In looking at a solution, you are engaging with positive emotions and are more likely to have (and trigger) positive emotions. You are asking for the results and outcomes you want to experience. If you waved a magic wand and the problems were resolved, what would it look like? That is what we would call being solution focused. In focusing on a problem, you are looking at negativity and are more likely to feel (and trigger) fear, anger, or defensiveness. This becomes a self-defeating spiral, because when we are talking about the problem, we are perceived as snipping, criticizing, being negative. Eventually other people tune us out. This is what we would call being problem focused.

For example, Joan, a coaching client of mine, made this shift in her focus during our work together. I watched Joan go from being someone who complained bitterly about her boss's behavior (always criticizing him and his decision making) to instead asking for what she wanted from him. Joan stopped focusing on his blind spots and began to see his strengths. Instead of complaining, she started describing solutions and what the situation would look like if things were going well. She involved him where his strengths would play out best and told him how she was involving others where she needed different abilities. This shift in Joan transformed her relationship with her boss and rippled into creating more meaningful conversations in every area of her life.

When people fight about something, the subject of the argument is rarely the real issue. The real issue is about vulnerability,

11

connectedness, safety, trust, or love—which are all emotional states. We connect with others authentically, with deep rapport and emotional safety, when we listen to ourselves well enough to tap into our own thoughts and feelings and share them in the moment. Then when we listen to others, we create the space for them to be here now, emotionally engaged. That's being emotionally intelligent.

Emotional Wake and Changing the Focus

An "emotional wake" is the feeling we leave people with. When we leave a meeting, are team members consistently feeling angry because they were not heard? Or are they feeling hopeful about what the team is working on? The predominant emotion we leave people with is our emotional wake.

Can you think of someone who creates a positive emotional wake? I bet someone comes to mind immediately. Being around that person feels good. Consciously or unconsciously, this person decided to be solution focused instead of problem focused in the face of change. Doing this creates respect for self and others.

Well-meaning colleagues or team members may want to dig a little for information by asking, "How is your boss?" when they know he is stressed due to recently announced changes. It is up to each of us to know ourselves and to know whether or not this is a topic we want to discuss now. If that is not where you want to take yourself emotionally at this time, it is no personal affront against the other person. Considering these options is being aware of your emotional wake. Be aware of your own needs and boundaries by being emotionally literate in the moment.

Having the emotional intelligence to deal with our own emotions first gives us the confidence and ability to navigate through the changes that are inevitable in our work and careers. We can experience an emotional hijack as a result of a change, or we can self-regulate and catch ourselves before we head into an emotional uproar. We can be aware of how other people's emotions are impacting their ability to have a meaningful conversation during times of change. When we know how to process ourselves and others through our emotions, we will be able to create more meaningful conversations consistently no matter how big the changes.

Here are some examples of how it sounds when people are able to understand the importance of their emotional wake and change a conversation's focus.

Scott and Alex

Scott and Alex met to discuss doing a deal together. Scott proposed some ideas that triggered the feeling of joy for Alex. Some of the symptoms of joy for Alex included being visibly excited, seeing lots of possibilities, imagining inevitable success, and ignoring red flags that might indicate a need to slow down and listen closely. Alex agreed to move forward with the project during their conversation due to the excitement he felt. Alex verbally committed to investing money and time in Scott's project.

Once back in his own office and the joyful feeling had passed, Alex was then able to think clearly and evaluate the key messages of Scott's proposal. He recognized questions he should have asked before agreeing to move forward. Alex wrote in his journal about the triggers and symptoms that the joy created in him so that next time he could catch himself before being caught up in the emotional rush. He decided the next time he felt that kind of joy, he was going to notice the feeling but not get so swept up in it that he agreed to spend money or time while in the first blush of the emotional high.

Bruno

In another situation with emotional implications, a well-respected and well-known pharmaceutical company had just announced that it would be laying off a large number of employees. As a result, one of the directors, Bruno, called me to discuss the fear he was feeling. This is how our conversation flowed:

Bruno: *As a result of the layoff announcement, I notice that my thinking is mistrustful of communication from leadership and peers. I am not sure whom to believe anymore. I am bouncing off the walls. I wonder if they*

13

*are considering eliminating my role and my team. I am afraid to speak
to anyone.*

Shawn: *Feeling fear in this situation is normal, Bruno. As soon as we
experience something that threatens our work, money, title, safety, family, or sense of self, it is normal to feel fear. What you are experiencing
now are your symptoms of fear. It is useful to take a deep breath and
observe your thoughts, body, and mood. When a crisis is occurring or
perceived to be on the horizon, it can be difficult to create meaningful
dialogue and new possibilities because we are not at our best. In my years
of research and observation, it has become clear that every professional
and every organization experiences problems that trigger fear. It is how
we deal with fear that makes the difference. Can you think of a previous
experience in which you felt fear and handled it well? Perhaps you created something even better for yourself and others?*

Bruno: *Yes.*

Shawn: *What did you do in that situation when you handled fear well
and created something better from it?*

Bruno: *I talked openly to my manager about what I was experiencing;
I looked him in the eye and asked him if he would keep me updated on
what was happening. When he said he would, I felt better. I admitted
that no one is in control of what will happen tomorrow. Also, I created a
Plan B for myself. I thought out what I would do if I did not have the
job, so that if I lost my job I'd have ideas about how to proceed and not
go into shock or shut down.*

Shawn: *Is there a leader in the company you could reach out to and look
in the eye to open a dialogue about your feelings, asking to use this situation as an opportunity to build trust?*

Bruno: *Yes, I can call her. Not sure she is in the office today, but I can
reach out to initiate a conversation.*

Shawn: *Good. I look forward to hearing how that conversation goes.
Bruno, this is also an opportunity for you to deepen the trust you have
with your own team. What can you do for your team of employees,
recognizing that some of them may be feeling fear too? What could you
do to help them feel trust in your communication with them? How can
you help to keep them focused on the current goals despite the emotional
roller coaster they may be experiencing?*

Bruno: *I can't tell them that their jobs are safe since I do not know what is happening yet myself. But I can give them my word to communicate with them as soon as I am able to do so. I can also share with them what I am working on as my top priorities and ask them to tell me what they are focused on today. I can show respect for what they are experiencing by reaching out and listening rather than avoiding them. I can ask how I could be supportive today even though I do not have all the answers now.*

Shawn: *Sounds like a good next step. Bruno, you also mentioned when you handled a similar fear well in the past that you created a Plan B for yourself. Would you like to talk through your Plan B ideas after you have had some time to think about that? Would you begin to keep a list of creative options that you would explore if you were told that your position was being eliminated? It would be good for you if some of the ideas were playful too. What is a creative, fun option that comes to mind now? What would you enjoy creating?*

Bruno: *Well, I have wanted to go to Europe with my wife. I've noticed there are some great prices on cruises now, and just the other day we were talking about how much fun that would be. That idea does not take care of what I'd do for work, but it is fun to think about where we could go and what we'd do. I'd really like to do the Eastern Mediterranean cruise because each of those stops looks great. We also enjoy cruise ships with all the various forms of entertainment.*

Shawn: *Bruno, notice how your voice just changed. I bet you just slipped out of fear as you were speaking about that vacation.*

Bruno: *Yes, I did. I feel hopeful about having a great vacation.*

Shawn: *Are you willing to play with that idea a bit more today? It is from that hopeful energy that lots of new possibilities will flow that will help you see new ways to deal with your current situation.*

Bruno: *Yes, I already feel lighter. The reality is the same, but my thinking and feelings have shifted. I can see how I will be able to think about new creative ideas from this mindset. Thanks for helping me process myself through the initial fear reaction.*

Bruno realized that his own emotional awareness and his ability to move through fear are foundational to navigating the changes he is experiencing at work.

Collin and Jake

This next example of the importance of being aware of how our emotional wake impacts our conversations focuses on Collin, an environmental scientist for the Environmental Protection Agency. He was transferred into a new role that required his family to move across the country. His excitement about the new position was obvious. His new job was to be the backup technician for the other specialists in the lab. This new role required each of the team members to train Collin to use the instrumentation in their labs. Collin's new manager, Jake, asked the other team members to train Collin but did not offer any incentive for them to do so.

A few days after Jake asked the team members to train Collin, none of them had reached out to Collin to show him around their labs. Eager to be proactive, Collin went into Sue's lab and said he'd like to learn to use the equipment. She said, "No, this week isn't good for me. It would be best for you to go work with someone else. I don't need your help." Later, he overheard her say to another of the lab scientists, "I don't know why you would want to train someone else to do your job. I'm not going to teach Collin how to use my equipment so he can replace me or mess up my experiments when I am out of the lab." Sue and the other team members were feeling fear. Whenever fear takes over, thinking logic shuts down. As a result, none of the team members were eagerly inviting Collin into their lab.

Jake is a hands-off manager who does not appear to be aware that fear of Collin's real reason for being there is preventing progress. The team members are not feeling safe enough or emotionally literate enough to talk through their own fears. For Collin to be successful in his new role, he will have to be emotionally intelligent and use strong social skills to create a Conversation for Connection (see Chapter 5) that addresses their feelings and creates safety that he is not going to take their jobs or mess up their experiments. Collin also needs to create a conversation with Jake to share what he is experiencing and ask Jake to address the team members' fears and provide incentives for the lab technicians to include him.

Barry and Jamal

Barry is a project manager in a mid-sized company. He shared with me, "When speaking with someone who has significantly more experience and know-how in an area than I do, I've noticed sometimes that I hesitate to ask questions." We discussed why this might be happening, and Barry was able to identify the underlying emotion—fear. Barry was able to point to a specific example when this happened recently. He was working with another project manager, Jamal, who had been developing a software design project for about a year. Barry had just joined the team and had six questions or points he did not understand after reading the current project plan. He was hesitant to ask Jamal about these. Barry was stuck in a conversation with himself thinking about the best way to ask Jamal so as not to annoy him or appear to be dumb.

Barry's communication style causes him to prefer to verbalize his thinking in order to really understand what it is he is mulling over. As an extrovert, he has to say it out loud to know what he is really thinking and feeling. Barry realized that speaking about when he is jammed up or stuck emotionally makes all the difference. He talked this out with Ali, a colleague. She listened to him as he shared what he was thinking and how he was hesitating. That is when he was able to identify the underlying feeling as fear. He was then able to change his conversation to focus instead on what he wanted to create.

Ali asked great self-awareness questions like the ones shared earlier in the chapter about how to process yourself through an emotion. After Barry spoke with Ali, he realized he was unstuck. He saw clearly that he was choosing this emotional state of fear and that he could choose something else, like hope, which would be more productive in creating a motivating conversation with Jamal. Barry was then able to ask Jamal his questions without coming from a position of fear. This changed the outcomes he created with Jamal.

Moving past that fear gave Barry the confidence to ask more clarifying questions without worrying that he might appear

17

dumb or annoy Jamal. Barry said to me, "I've noticed recently I am now able to process myself through stuck spots like that. It's as if I can hear the questions Ali would ask me and think it out or write it out in my journal."

Emotions motivate our actions. When we identify what we are feeling in the moment, we can be self-aware and begin to regulate our emotions intentionally. This gives us the ability to catch ourselves and others when we are stuck. We can intentionally process ourselves and others through a stuck emotion that is holding us back. We are more productive in conversations when we know how to do this. Being aware of the emotional wake we are leaving with others creates better working relationships. When we know what motivates others, we can focus on creating conversations that will inspire and move toward creating the results we desire. Emotions and values are linked together because what we value will trigger our emotions. Our values guide where we want to focus our energy and what we want to talk about. It is this connection that we will explore next.

Values: Workplace Motivators

Professional relationships constantly change, especially in new settings or under new conditions. The glue that keeps people and organizations together is their values. Understanding one another's values helps us build rapport and create meaningful connections.

Cara was a star performer on the high-potential track in the huge accounting firm where she worked for over 10 years. Every 12 to 18 months she was given increased responsibility or a promotion. She enjoyed serving as the controller and aspired to be the chief financial officer (CFO). Cara also served on the board of a nonprofit organization and helped that organization revamp its processes and solved some complex problems the organization had been struggling with for many years. Cara felt great about her career and her potential. When the president of the nonprofit organization invited Cara to be the new CFO, she was excited. The first few months in her new role proved to be more difficult than Cara imagined it would be. And a year into the new position, Cara was asked to resign from her role. What happened? How could she go from being a high-performing star in one organization and asked to resign in a short time from another?

Our values or workplace motivators determine what we want to talk about. We will be interested in creating conversations that align with our values. Likewise, we will move away from or be resistant to conversations that are focused on topics that we do not value. Cara first worked in an accounting organization that deeply valued return on investment, problem solving, and rules. These values matched Cara's workplace motivators. She moved into a nonprofit organization that was mainly focused on helping people, making sure that people felt good about themselves, and being the recognized leader in charitable work. The values of the new organization were not a good fit for Cara's workplace motivators.

The Six Basic Workplace Values

In my coaching work, one of the assessments I use with my clients focuses on *values*, also described as "workplace motivators." According to research done by Eduard Spranger in *Types of Men* (1928) and later G. W. Allport in *The Study of Values* (1960), there are six basic values that show up in the workplace. These are:

1. *Utilitarian.* Wanting things to be useful and productive, seeking financial well-being; possibly using money or points to keep score. This value is all about practicality and return on investment.
2. *Aesthetic.* Wanting things to feel good, look good, or sound pleasing; artistic, creative, subjective.
3. *Theoretical.* Wanting the answers, facts, data, and truth and sharing knowledge.
4. *Traditional.* Wanting instructions or procedures so that life can be lived or work can be done correctly.
5. *Social.* Wanting to make a difference for others, wanting to solve people issues, such as hate, poverty, homelessness, hunger, and political issues.
6. *Individualistic.* Wanting to be at the table when decisions

are made, seeking to be an expert whose voice matters, winning and leading in a world-class way.

Each of us is motivated by our top two values; they determine why we do what we do. Both our top values and our lowest values have a huge impact on our best career path, culture, and success pattern and the types of conversations we find meaningful. We will discuss how these top two values impact our career choices in more detail later in this chapter.

Our values are the glue that keeps us connected. When our values match up well with a boss, a team, or an organizational culture, we thrive. We know what to focus on in conversation. When we share our own values with others in what we are doing, we show up as authentic. We experience satisfaction, joy, hope, and love when we are clear on our values and are making choices that are aligned with them.

Let's explore each of the six values more in depth so we can begin to identify them in ourselves or others.

Utilitarian

People with high utilitarian values want a return on their investment of time, energy, and money. Self-made people who create new products and services for a profit have high utilitarian values. In her book *Secrets of Millionaire Moms*, author Tamara Monosoff shares how moms turned great ideas into booming businesses. This topic would appeal to someone who has high utilitarian values, who is driven to succeed financially.

A well-known utilitarian, Ayn Rand, wrote a series of books based on her philosophy, "American's abundance was not created by public sacrifices to the public good but by the productive genius of free men who pursued their own personal interests and the making of their own private fortunes." This ethos is appealing to someone with high utilitarian values.

Professional organizers are typically driven by utilitarian values. They want to make an impact on how their clients use space, time, and resources. Cynthia Kyriazis is a professional organizer who is able to create meaningful conversations about the use of paper, time, and space. She transforms people's lives as a result of the conversations she creates by asking about how they organize their time, space, and paper to fulfill their goals. Her know-how makes her look almost telepathic to someone who does not have the ability to read people's values through conversation. It is her high utilitarian value that drives or motivates Cynthia to make an impact in such practical ways.

High utilitarian values are the foundation for successful careers such as:

- Salesperson
- Entrepreneur
- Financial officer
- Professional organizer
- Banker

Aesthetic

When someone has high aesthetic values, he or she will want things to feel good, look good, or sound pleasing. Some children develop this value at an early age and begin to show signs of artistic, design, or musical ability. Others may develop this value later in life as other values have been fulfilled. When the aesthetic value is highest, a person will put a strong emphasis on form, function, feelings, and the need to be in environments that are beautiful and harmonious to their senses.

Martha Stewart's business is all about the aesthetic focus and appeals to people who value beauty and harmony. Cooking, interior design, flower arranging, wedding planning, and catering were all early interests for Martha. She also has a healthy dose of utilitarian in her own values profile, which is what drove her to create the business empire she now leads.

When I graduated from college, I had two roommates who were chefs in a very prestigious restaurant. They worked very different hours than my more traditional 8-to-5 day job. In the wee hours of the night they would arrive home from work and begin to cook their own masterpiece for dinner. I ate incredible foods for breakfast during that time. One night I listened as they banged around in the kitchen and discussed salmon—everything about salmon. For close to two hours, every sentence they spoke had to do with salmon. I began to wonder whether I was dreaming. When I got up, they served me several salmon dishes that were amazing creations. Not only did they taste wonderful, but they were beautiful to look at. Each plate was an artistic creation. This conversation was deeply engaging for them as they both had aesthetic as their highest value, whereas it was almost incomprehensible for me since aesthetic was my lowest value.

High aesthetic values are the foundation for successful careers such as:

- Interior designer
- Musician
- Artist
- Physical trainer
- Landscaper
- Chef
- Hair stylist
- Photographer

Theoretical

A person who enjoys reading, doing research, solving problems, and working with facts, data, and logic is having fun because of his or her high theoretical value. Reading a series of books on a specific topic and watching documentaries on PBS are also likely common activities for this values type. Passion for education and learning are signs that someone is driven by this value.

Oprah Winfrey tells stories of her own childhood and how much she enjoyed reading. She created a school in Africa, a magazine, and a book club all based on her high value for the theoretical. Oprah enjoys creating conversations that have a theoretical thread in them.

High theoretical values are the foundation for successful careers such as:

- Professor
- Scientist
- Investigator
- Doctor
- Researcher
- Mathematician

Traditional

Have you ever observed someone who has a system for living? Living by a set of rules and encouraging others to accept the same standards is common for someone with high traditional values. These rules could be a strong focus on quality processes, laws, procedures, or religious doctrine.

Political activists and fundamental religious groups are often known for pushing their views on others aggressively. This is a signal that they are operating from the traditional value; however, that level of aggressiveness does not show up in every person who is motivated by the traditional value. There are plenty of others who come from a traditional motivation and who help people each day.

High traditional values are the foundation for successful careers such as:

- Quality control expert
- Teacher or trainer
- Pastor
- Wedding planner
- Funeral director
- Firefighter
- Police officer

Social

Have you ever been part of a group that was focused on doing something for others, such as working with Habitat for Humanity, for example? Wanting to make a difference for others—wanting to solve social issues such as hate, poverty, homelessness, and political issues—is a clue that someone has high social values.

Most nonprofit organizations, such as the United Way, Kiva, and the Red Cross, were started by people with social values as their primary motivator. For-profit companies can also be driven by the social value. When you see an organization that puts the welfare of people above its desire to make a profit, you are seeing the social value in action. Johnson & Johnson is a company well known for how it handled the 1982 Tylenol tampering incidents when the company recalled millions of dollars of products and placed the safety of its customers ahead of its financial bottom line, demonstrating its commitment to people first.

High societal values are the foundation for successful careers such as:

- Teacher or trainer
- Firefighter
- Police officer
- Emergency medical technician
- Fund-raiser
- Nonprofit employee

Individualistic

When you see someone who enjoys leading groups, teams, or committees, you are seeing signs of the individualistic value in action. Wanting to win, wanting to be at the table when decisions are made, and seeking to be an expert whose voice matters are indications that you are looking at someone with high individualistic values. People who become household names because of their own drive typically have this value in the top three. Corporate and political leaders have in common the individualistic value; otherwise they would not be willing to do what it takes to stay in a leadership role. The individualistic value is a drive that will cause people to stand up for change. When they see how something could be done better, they are willing to initiate changes to make it happen.

High individualistic values are the foundation for successful careers as:

- CEO
- President
- Committee Chairperson
- Politician
- Leaders of associations and organizations

Your Top Two Values

You can tell a lot about people's values from their career choices, and vice versa. Let's take the individualistic value and explore it a bit more. If it is in the top three values, it will drive a person to want to be a leader. Unlike the other values, the individualistic value is expressed through the two other values that are close to it on a ranked list of values. In other words, if "individualistic" is in the top two or three values, it acts as a booster to the two that are next to it in the list. So, for example, imagine that Andy's values were ranked in this order:

1. Individualistic
2. Theoretical
3. Social
4. Traditional
5. Utilitarian
6. Aesthetic

Someone with the individualistic value above the theoretical and social may want to become a highly regarded professor at an Ivy League university, or perhaps an award-winning television documentary producer focused on helping people by disseminating cutting-edge information. Individualistic adds the motivation to step out, to lead, and to be part of what is considered to be the best or world class.

As another example, Alice's top two values rank looks like this:

1. Aesthetic
2. Individualistic

She could be motivated to become an award-winning architect, an interior designer, a yoga instructor, a psychologist, or a world-class art collector. The third value on her list will determine which of those paths would be better for her. If she has utilitarian as her third value, she will be driven to earn more money than if she had social as her third value, which would motivate her to want to help people through a meaningful cause.

Our Values Impact Our Conversations

So why is all this information about values so important to meaningful conversations that focus important change? There are two reasons. First of all, as Judy Suiter, CEO of Competitive Edge Inc., puts it: "If you do not know what your values and priorities are, someone else will determine them for you."

In order for us to be able to have our own agenda with goals and motivation, we need to understand ourselves. Our values determine what we are motivated to do. Having a private conversation with ourselves about what our own values are is the first step in this awareness. Review the results of your own values assessment, and think about how your values have motivated the choices you've made about your work and your relationships with bosses and teams. Identify the times in your career when you were not motivated. This is likely because the rewards of the project, organization, or boss did not align to your own top three values. As we understand the impact our values have had on our own motivation, we can begin to see the impact values have on other people. You can ask questions of others to understand their values. When you have a sense of what someone else's values are, you will be able to initiate conversations focused on topics that would be of interest to them.

The second reason it is important to understand values is that in order to impact change, you will need to be able to identify the value motivators of the people and organizations you are working with. Corporate cultures have a values profile that focuses the work of the organization. Omnimedia, the company run by Martha Stewart, has aesthetic, utilitarian, and theoretical values as its core. If you work with that organization, you'd need to be able to connect to these values. Martha Stewart herself probably has high individualistic, aesthetic, and utilitarian values that drove her to be as famous and powerful as she is. Understanding the difference between the values of the individual and the values of the organization helps us to communicate clearly. Having the awareness to see the values between an organization and an individual also helps us to know where and with whom we would fit in best.

People with high traditional and social values will feel like they are beating their head against a brick wall if they go to work in an organization that is driven by utilitarian and theoretical values. This is a conversation I frequently have with my coaching clients. We identify their values hierarchy and the values hierarchy of the organization in which they work so we understand how well they fit in as well as where their tricky spots will be. When your core workplace motivators match the organization's values, it is more likely you will experience joy in your work. For example, Ali worked in an architectural firm where the top core values of the organization were aesthetic and theoretical. Ali's top values are social and utilitarian. She did not feel recognized or rewarded for her contributions and suggestions. When she realized this, she decided to make a career change to an organization that would reward her passion for social and utilitarian projects.

Your values hierarchy impacts how you make decisions. Think about the conversations you have had that changed the direction of your own life. What have been the turning point conversations in your own life?

You can observe other people's values by asking them what they are passionate about, where they put their time, resources, and money. "What do you do that makes you feel most alive?" is a great question to uncover what someone values. Alice, a human resources director, often invites people in her division to participate in the organization's United Way drive or the Habitat for Humanity day. She does this with joy because it mirrors her high social value. If you wanted to get to know Alice better, start by asking her a few questions about one of these projects. She'll be delighted to engage in a conversation about the impact working with Habitat for Humanity has had on several of the teams in her organization.

Conversations change when relationships change. When college interns at my company move from being college students to full-time employees, or when clients move from one company to another, conversations change. A former college intern of mine rarely initiates a conversation for planning the structure of her career now that we do not see each other as often. Instead our conversations are more social. When a long-time client moves on to a new organization and wants to bring me in to work with her, our conversation changes. We begin with a new Conversation for Connection (discussed in Chapter 5) focused on the new company, even though we would not have done so when she was working with her former company since we spoke several times each week then. Because relationships change, we need to know how to build new relationships that will be meaningful and effective for both parties.

This process doesn't simply begin when you're introduced to the working world. Young people form their values on the playground, in the classroom, and at birthday parties, and they will hone a values hierarchy and values ranking by somewhere around 20 years old. After that our values hierarchy will only change if we have significant emotional events. Some examples of significant emotional events include being promoted into a new role that is a huge leap, losing a loved one through death or divorce, and experiencing the birth of a child or grandchild. These significant emotional experiences create a window where we reevaluate what is important to us, and we may shift our values hierarchy as a result.

Based on observation of our 20-year-old marketing intern, Alex, I know that his top two values are utilitarian and individualistic. If Alex allows his values to motivate his decision, he'll create a career path to own his own business or lead a division of a business. Our other intern, Don, has high aesthetic and social values. He majored in economics and entrepreneurship, although he shows no motivation in that direction. He may be building his ladder against the wrong wall for him to experience meaning and happiness in his work.

Steve, the vice president of operations in a pharmaceutical company, was downsized from a role in which he felt like he was beating his head against a wall. His top two values are social and traditional. If he lets his values motivate his direction, he may decide that now is the time to follow a lifelong dream he has had of being a pastor, where both his top two values would be rewarded by the work.

Values or workplace motivators will point to the topics a person would be willing to listen to. For example, someone with a high utilitarian value will enjoy talking about making money. Someone with low utilitarian would be turned off by that conversation. If you want to get someone interested in a conversation, you've got to connect to his or her top two values. Ask questions that get people to talk about their passions, and you will be able to tell what their top values are.

It is much easier to connect with people, companies, and situations that will build momentum and growth when we maintain self-awareness about who we really are. When we choose bosses, career paths, and organizations that respect our top two values, we have the best chance of offering what we naturally bring to the table and, hence, are provided with good opportunities to succeed.

The topics that will be most engaging to us and the areas in which we want to engage with others will be driven by our own values. Knowing our own values highlights the types of conversations that will be most meaningful for us. Being able to identify someone else's values will show us what he or she would be interested in talking about. Once you know what people are interested in talking about, you can begin to figure out what their preferred communication style is and how they will approach a conversation.

Communication Styles

Jonathan, the president of a mid-sized university, invited me to observe one of his advisory board meetings because he said he was "stumped by the team dynamics going on with this group of people." As I observed their meetings, I noticed that when a team member, Mike, spoke, no one seemed to pay attention. But a few minutes later in the meeting, when another team member, Kim, made the same point using different words and another example, everyone seemed to be engaged, agreeing to move forward with the idea. Every time Kim made a suggestion, the group would agree and build on what she said. Every time Mike made a suggestion, it was as if he had plopped the idea out there, and everyone dismissed it. Jonathan told me that he had appointed Mike to this board because they worked together on another board and Mike had made significant contributions to that team. Why was this dynamic happening?

In short, it all comes down to adapting to preferred communication styles. Who do you know that is masterful in communicating with a variety of people? I often ask this question in presentations. Frequent answers are Oprah Winfrey, Bill Clinton, Ronald Reagan, and Anderson Cooper. People who are known for being outstanding communicators know how to say what other people need to hear in a way they can hear it. They know how to spot different communication needs. They understand the different communication styles and why each one adds value to the whole effort. They behave in a way that says one communication style is not better or worse than another. In fact, we know successful businesses are led by CEOs from all the various communication styles.

Our preferred communication style determines how we will approach a meaningful conversation. Kim's communication style was very similar to most of the other board members'. Mike's style, on the other hand, was 180 degrees away from that of the majority of the board members on Jonathan's advisory board.

The Communications-Style Assessments

In my work as an executive coach, I use assessments that show a person's preferred communication style, workplace motivators, emotional intelligence, and natural talent. These four individual assessments are the foundation for coaching, team development, and organizational structure design and also form the basis for the work I do with teams. In addition, these assessments help individuals to understand their own leadership style and method of building relationships with others. They are powerful because they raise awareness about both the individual and the team as a whole. This awareness enables communication to occur more intentionally and clearly. For the purposes of this chapter, we are focused now on understanding preferred communication styles.

One of the many benefits of using these assessments is that they show a person's preferred style and adapted style. We all have a preferred way of communicating using our natural talents. Some people do not feel that they need to adapt their communication style in order to be successful. Other people, however, feel they need to adapt their natural preference in order to be accepted at work and in professional relationships. The assessment shows if a person is adapting who he or she is to "fit in." All of us adapt at certain times, especially as we learn how to use our know-how about styles to communicate effectively. Still, when someone is making a significant adaptation to how he or she normally behaves, it can be stressful and detrimental to long-term success.

In conversations some people prefer to answer questions that begin with the word *what,* focusing on the big-picture concept. Others prefer to answer questions that are focused on *how* and the step-by-step approach to doing something. Still others would rather start with *why* and the rationale for taking action. Your boss may prefer to make decisions during a conversation and gets an energy boost from doing so, whereas one of your peers may feel terribly uncomfortable making snap decisions and needs a few days to mull over the pros and cons before making the decision. One of your team members may need to verbalize ideas so she knows what she is thinking, while another prefers to think things out alone. How do you know someone's preferred communication style? By "people-reading," you will be able to identify an individual's communication preference. Understanding preferred communication is foundational to all conversations.

Predictable clusters of behaviors fit together and impact a person's approach to communication. For example, the statement "I am going *to research* before I make a recommendation" can mean very different things to different people. Take Carl, for instance. When Carl says, "I am going to research the options," he means he is going to find every possible option, do a comprehensive search, deeply explore and read about all the possibilities, create a pro-and-con list, and maybe even e-mail someone who has experienced each option to confirm his understanding. But to another person, let's call him Paul, this means he is going to find something (maybe a sign) that indicates that his idea has merit and that what his gut feeling is telling him is worth pursuing. When Paul finds one article that confirms his idea is a good one, he is confident in his decision and ready to move forward. That is his "research." If Carl and Paul are talking to each other, they may find communication frustrating if they do not understand the range of style preferences. Paul will think Carl bogs things down and takes too much time to do his work. Carl will think Paul is not trustworthy because he did not really research the way Carl does, and Carl believes Paul is just winging it most of the time.

If Paul and Carl understand communication styles, they will play to the strengths of their styles and cover each other's blind spots. In other words, they may agree that Carl will spend three days coming up with the option he can find. Carl will share that with Paul so he has the big picture. Carl will also understand that Paul likely already knows his gut reaction, and he is looking at the data to see if he can move forward now with this idea. On the third day they can meet to discuss Carl's findings and then together in the meeting make a decision they can both live with. Because of Paul's preferred style, he will likely make connections with people and concepts that Carl would not naturally see. Paul will be able to sell the concept to others and get them engaged in bringing the idea alive.

Until we have learned how to work with all the communication styles, we are most likely to build natural rapport with people whose communication style is most like our own. If people have a communication style that is opposite ours, unless we understand this, it will be challenging to understand their intentions and where they are coming from. We may see our differences as problems rather than the opportunity to cover one another's blind spots. For example, Nancy, one of my clients, received some feedback from her boss and peers saying she was defensive most of the time. Nancy was shocked by this feedback because she did not feel defensive. What might be going on here? Nancy's communication style is one that likes facts, data, and logic. Nancy thinks in a logical, fact-based manner all the time. Her boss and peers have the exact opposite communication style. They are very emotional and do what they want to do when they want to do it, with little regard for a step-by-step plan with logic or research. When someone with their communication style is backed into a corner and needs to defend himself or herself, that is when the person will go get the logical facts. Nancy's boss assumes Nancy is behaving as he would. He is applying his own communication style to her behavior, and he is 100 percent off the mark about what her behavior means.

Have you ever received feedback that felt completely off the mark to you? Chances are that you and the person giving the feedback had very different communication styles and neither of you were aware of this.

The Four Communication Styles

Imagine there are four windows in a huge room. When you look out of one window, you see a beach scene complete with waves crashing and children building sand castles. When you pivot and look out another window, you see a city scene with high-rise business buildings, great restaurants, and lots of taxis. When you look out of the third window, you see a mountain scene with snow, ski runs, and a lodge that looks like it serves great hot chocolate. Finally, you look out of the fourth window, and you see a camping ground next to a lake and wild animals. Depending on which window or windows you are looking out, you would answer the question "What would you like to do today?" differently. This is a metaphor for what is happening in every conversation we have, as people are looking out of their own communication-style window or windows.

> We see the world not as it is, but as we are.
> —Stephen Covey

Some people prefer to look out one window exclusively, whereas others look out two or three windows at one time. There are four primary windows and sixty combinations of windows. It is useful to start with a strong understanding of the four primary windows first. Once you understand them very well, then the other combinations will make more sense.

Before I explain the four communication styles, I think it is important to point out that there is no right one. Each style has strengths and blind spots. The goal is to understand our own

37

communication preference first and then to understand the bigger picture of each of the communication-style preferences so we understand where other people, individually or in groups, are coming from in their own communication.

To thank you for reading this book, I would like to give you a complementary assessment so you understand your own preferred communication style. If you would like to complete an online assessment that shows you your own communication style profile, please go to www.TheProfessionalDevelopment-Group.com. You will need to provide your e-mail address so that your report can be e-mailed to you.

Special Bonus Offer!

To complete your online assessment, please go to www.The ProfessionalDevelopmentGroup.com and click on the Talent Mastery Assessments button on the left. Then click on the Take Assessments button. Use response link 124439XUB.

The four communication styles are Dominant, Influential, Steady, and Compliant (DISC). Each has its own cluster of predictable behaviors. Once you notice two or three of these tendencies in a person, you can count on the others being there too.

High Dominant Style

The High Dominant style has these behavioral characteristics:
- Likes challenges and a fast pace
- Wants to control the agenda
- Is good at handling problems and challenges
- Relies on gut instinct
- Is very active and can be perceived by the other styles as being aggressive in getting results

- Goes directly at conflict or problems with no fear
- Will take risks that other styles would not consider
- Is quick to challenge others and likes a back-and-forth debate (may be seen by other styles as argumentative)
- Loves to win
- Does not like repetitive work and dislikes not being able to make decisions
- Fears being taken advantage of
- Likes to initiate change for self and others
- Reduces stress by working out, engaging in competitive physical activity
- Needs to learn humility
- Makes quick decisions (will say yes or no quickly)

The High Dominant Style is drawn to:
- Luxury options
- Professionalism
- Power to make decisions
- Status symbols
- Customized solutions

When speaking with a High Dominant–style person, frame your ideas this way:
- "We can make this happen if we decide today . . ."
- "The results we are aiming for . . ."
- "We can be the best or the first at this if we . . ."
- "The bottom-line benefits are . . ."
- "Let's take action on this now . . ."
- "Let's pick up the pace on this . . ."

When talking with a High Dominant–style person, avoid:
- Getting thrown off if the person seems confrontational. Instead, come into the conversation with the same candid up-front energy, and he or she will respect you.
- Moving slowly or insisting on talking about every detail.

- Walking on eggshells, afraid the person will explode—High Dominants might express their feelings with intensity, but stay with them through the conversation and they will be able to let it go quicker than other styles let go of issues.

High Influence Style

The High Influence style has these behavioral characteristics:

- Likes to interact and persuade others to his or her point of view
- Is good at including others, interacting with others, selling ideas
- Is outgoing and social
- Trusts others easily
- Is very enthusiastic and optimistic and does not want to focus on topics that bring him or her down
- Is a creative problem solver, especially involving people
- Is great at networking
- Is fun loving and impulsive
- Can be perceived by other styles as insincere because he or she is so friendly to everyone
- Does not like pessimism, negativity, or skepticism
- Fears not being liked
- May not notice changes going on around him or her
- Reduces stress by going to a social event, talking with people he or she likes
- Needs to learn self-discipline
- Makes quick, impulsive decisions and will appreciate creative new possibilities

The High Influence style is drawn to:

- Showy, flashy, new trends
- Fun
- Creativity

- Attention
- Social standing

When speaking with a High Influence–style person, frame your ideas this way:
- "I'm excited we are going to . . ."
- "Imagine this . . ."
- "So many people will . . ."
- "I feel so happy about . . ."
- "You'll win the chairman's club award if you . . ."
- "Wow, this is going to be fun . . ."
- "I love working with you because . . ."
- "This is great news! . . ."

When talking with a High Influence–style person, avoid:
- Using lots of facts, data, and logic to persuade.
- Getting frustrated when the person goes off on a tangent. Just bring him or her back to the conversation at hand.
- Expecting him or her to stick with detailed, complex, long-term projects (High Influencers need variety).

High Steady Style

The High Steady style has these behavioral characteristics:
- Likes security and steadiness
- Is good at creating the pace or process for self and others
- Likes to create short-term plans
- Prefers having clear directions and guidelines for work and activities
- Wants to know how things will be done step-by-step
- Is good at listening and is able to calm others
- Masks own emotions (other styles may find High Steadies hard to read emotionally)
- Has great patience and will stick it out through difficult times
- Needs own space

- Does not like lack of closure or inability to complete a task
- Fears loss of stability and conflict
- Gets overwhelmed with fast change, needs time to adjust to change
- Reduces stress by having alone downtime like yard work or a hot bath
- Needs to learn self-confidence
- Is a methodical decision maker

Someone with a High Steady style is drawn to:
- Family activities
- Comfort
- Cozy, homey spaces
- Proven, tested assurances
- Safety
- Tradition

When speaking with a High Steady–style person, frame your ideas this way:
- "Let's take a few days and think this over before we make a decision."
- "We have a solid reputation for service and reliability."
- "Would you help me with . . . ?"
- "I promise I will . . ."
- "Take your time so you feel comfortable . . ."
- "We can make this happen on our own time schedule . . ."

When talking with a High Steady–style person, avoid:
- Pushing the person to make a decision quickly
- Expecting him or her to express disagreement directly or say no directly
- Getting to the big-picture concept in the first few minutes (it may take several conversations, but once High Steadies have the big-picture concept, they are able to stick with it longer than any other style)

High Compliance Style

**The High Compliance style has these
behavioral characteristics:**

- Likes accuracy and cautiousness
- Is good at creating policy and procedures and responding to rules set by others
- Can be perceived as too cautious by other styles
- May be overly critical of self and others
- Enjoys solving complex problems and thinking through details
- Analyzes and systematizes
- Has high expectations
- Expects others to follow the rules too
- Is troubled by risky situations and unscheduled events
- Does not like too much focus on emotions or feelings
- Fears criticism of work
- Will worry during times of change
- Reduces stress by having alone time to think
- Needs to learn to be more open verbally to share what is in his or her mind and heart
- Is a cautious decision maker

Someone with a High Compliance style will be drawn to:

- Conservative ideals
- Proven records
- High-quality standards
- Formality
- Privacy
- Measurable value and results

When speaking with a High Compliance–style person, use these phrasings:

- "The research shows . . ."
- "Would you analyze the data?"

- "There is no risk in us exploring these three options first . . ."
- "The facts are . . ."
- "There is a 90-day guarantee . . ."
- "This has a proven track record . . ."

When talking with a High Compliance–style person, avoid:
- Rushing the conversation, leaving little or no time for questions
- Asking for a personal opinion, gut reaction, or personal information
- Being emotional, random, or disorganized

Each person has a preference that includes looking out of one, two, or three of these communication styles. One or two styles tend to be used less than the others. The style we use less is the one that we likely have the most trouble with when we interact with people who choose that style as their preference.

Adapting to Other People's Communication Styles

When we are aware of our own preferences, we can make choices about when we adapt our style. If we are not aware of our own preferences, we may think others should adapt to us, or we may unconsciously adapt our style and appear to be wearing a mask. This can create a yo-yo–like behavior pattern that causes others to wonder if they are dealing with Dr. Jekyll and Mr. Hyde.

It's not what style you are, it is what you do
with your style that matters most.
—Bill Bonnstetter

I recently conducted the communication style assessments in a large corporate environment with the company's top 160 people. The team was led by a new CEO who wanted to get to know the staff and ascertain their abilities quickly. Two of the most senior people, who were now reporting directly to the CEO, had similar indications in the assessment reports I'd performed. They were both showing up with an adapted style that was 180 degrees away from who they preferred to be. In other words, their assessment reports showed someone with a High Influence style adapting to look like he has a High Compliance style.

My work in this situation was confidential, so as I met alone with the first of the two (let's call him John), I pointed out that the adaptation he was making in his communication style was severe and dramatic: He was not being himself. John said he did not know how to proceed because he thought the new CEO wanted him to be someone else, someone he knew he could not be. Predictably, he and the CEO were experiencing tremendous conflict during their meetings.

I suggested to John that he have a conversation with the new CEO and say, "I have not been being myself, and I apologize for this. I've been adapting to be what I thought you wanted from me. This is creating tremendous stress and will not serve either of us long term. I'd like to create a conversation with you about our preferred communication styles, workplace motivators, and natural talents so that we can play to each other's strengths, and so that I can support what you want to create."

When John met with his new boss and spoke these words, he altered the dynamics. The conversation changed for the better. John changed the foundation of their relationship. He was able to shift his behavior and choose his natural communication style in his work with his new boss. This created trust and momentum in their relationship. As a result of the courage John demonstrated in this conversation, there now was safety in their communication with each other.

The second individual (whom we'll call Steve) and I had a similar opening conversation. I shared his assessment results and pointed out that he was not being true to himself, to his natural style. Steve said that the CEO was unclear about what he wanted. To keep his job, Steve felt he had to disguise who he really was. He was not voicing his concerns or pointing out thoughtful observations he was having. Instead he was half-heartedly agreeing with whatever the CEO said. Steve was not adapting to the CEO's style to provide useful information that would help both of them get on the same page. He was having a recurring conversation in his own head:

> I need this job because I have a family to support, so I better do whatever my new boss expects of me or else I might be fired.

Steve was running this conversation over and over in his head as he sat in meetings with the new CEO. Steve was coming from an emotional state of fear and lacking. Steve was not able to self-regulate his emotions. He did not put himself in the shoes of the CEO, who was new to the role and had not yet figured out how the organization would be redesigned and what the roles of the key staff should be. Moreover, the CEO was trying to get to know the real Steve, but with the way things were going, he had no chance.

I suggested that Steve meet with his new boss and share with him what his preferred communication style really was and what his natural talents were. Steve said he could not do that because he knew the new CEO was too busy and would not have time for this type of dialogue. Instead, Steve stayed in his office waiting for the CEO to seek him out. I suspect that when they finally met, Steve's adapted style was so stressful for him that the new boss could sense something was off.

I received a phone call from Steve a month later saying he was no longer with the company. He said he was "ousted by the new CEO," who felt that Steve "was not the right fit for the team." I was sad but not all that surprised that Steve had created this outcome for himself because of the adapted communication style he was using.

A few days later, I spoke with the CEO, who told me he could not get a handle on who Steve was and he did not have time "to play cat and mouse trying to read him." Worse, he felt he could not *trust* Steve. There was no safety created in their communication for either of them.

A mentor of mine, Bill Bonnstetter, CEO of TTI Performance Systems, started researching DISC communication styles in 1979. He and his team have done in-depth research on the impact of style on buying patterns and people-reading. Bill shared with me that "the best way to sell our ideas or products is to identify the buyers' style before meeting with them. Prepare to communicate in their style using their language." When his team videotaped presentations, it was clear: When the style of the person who was proposing an idea matched the information needs of the buyer, the conversation flowed smoothly and there was less stress. When the style of the person proposing an idea did not match the information needs of the buyer, the stress level was visible and the questions were more challenging.

In a recent conversation, Bill Bonnstetter shared, "If I do not know the style of the person I am meeting with, I'd start the conversation as if they preferred a High Steady style. Forty percent of the population has a preference for the High Steady style. So I'd focus on reliability, guarantees, and consistency because that will appeal to someone with a High Compliance style too. Watch the body language to know how this is being heard." If you pay attention to your listener's body language, a person who has a High Dominant style will indicate the desire to move faster. If you see signs of this happening, you move to focus on the big picture and results and speed up the pace. If your people-reading indicates you need to shift to a High Compliance style, then focus on safety, low risk taking, and a task-oriented, detailed approach. If you sense you have someone whose preference is the High Influence style, that person will stick with you because he or she wants to be supportive, have fun, and connect on an emotional level. High Influencers want to know who else has bought into your idea or is using your product. Bill also suggests, "If you have someone with a High Compliance communication preference in a group audience, at the end of the meeting, say something like this, 'You probably have questions that I did not answer today. I'd like to leave you with my contact information so you can reach me if you have additional questions.'"

The DISC model of communication styles provides the best way of identifying how a person prefers to receive information. We are all hardwired in the way we like to receive communication. We can adapt our style to focus on how best to send information so that we blend our styles when needed.

People-reading is a skill that can be learned best by practicing. If this is a skill you want to master, then for the next 30 days, have one conversation each day with someone you do not know, and focus on identifying the person's preferred communication style, top values, and current emotion. Doing this will raise your awareness and take your interpersonal communication ability to the next level. In fact, you will dramatically change your own conversation ability by doing this. Another option if you want to improve your ability to read people is to attend my Talent@Work seminar. For details, check out www.TheProfessionalDevelopmentGroup.com.

> *Communicate with people in their language,*
> *from their point of view, in a language they understand.*
> —Terri Kabachnick, *I Quit but Forgot to Tell You*

Understanding our own emotions, workplace motivators, and communication-style preferences and how they impact others lays a strong foundation for meaningful communication. When the conversation needs to change, you can be the one who is willing to initiate the change. To have meaningful conversations, begin with knowing and understanding yourself. Then people-read others to explore the lenses they are using in their own communication. Remember, the core is emotional, then values (workplace motivators), then behavior (communication style). Understand what people are feeling currently, what triggers their passions, and how they want to approach communication, and you will create rapport and more meaning in your conversations.

You now have the foundation for understanding yourself and others so that you are able to create meaningful connections in conversation. Next we will explore the 12 conversations that you can use as building blocks to create momentum in your work and relationships.

PART II

THE 12 CONVERSATIONS

Overview of the 12 Conversations

The 12 conversations we are about to discuss are important for growth and success for leaders, managers, and teams. When we are comfortable creating each of these conversations, we experience confidence and credibility in our leadership style. When one or some of these conversations are missing from our dialogue with others, we will not create the success we are looking for. Missing conversations trip us and others up. As we've already discussed, great conversations are built on a foundation of awareness that includes emotional intelligence, what people want to talk about (motivators), and how they approach the communication (style.)

Each of the next chapters focuses on 1 of the 12 conversation types. Each type serves a different purpose in communication. Chances are good that you are already masterful in a few of these conversation types. And there may be a few of the conversation types that you avoid or do not know how to create. Before we break down the 12 conversations individually, though, let's have an overview. Below you will have the opportunity to rate yourself in various communication capabilities. From this rating you will be able to clearly see which of the conversations you already excel in and which ones you will want to practice. Consider this a prelearning check-in. You could come back again after reading the whole book as a way to identify how much you learned and where you want to focus your attention.

On a scale of 1 to 10, how masterful are you at creating each of these areas that impact conversations?

Rate your effectiveness in the following areas on a scale of 1–10 with 10 being very effective and 1 being ineffective										
	Ineffective							Very Effective		
	1	2	3	4	5	6	7	8	9	10
1. I understand the preferred communication style of the people I work closely with.										
2. I connect with people on an emotional level when needed.										
3. I share information about myself in order to deepen my connection with others.										
4. I engage in conversations to create and explore new ideas and possibilities.										
5. I brainstorm new ideas without judging or evaluating the idea too quickly.										
6. I consider a variety of options and encourage others on my team to join me.										
7. I develop clearly defined plans to meet my goals and objectives.										
8. I verbalize to team members how we will accomplish a goal.										
9. I have a system for tracking my progress on projects, goals, and initiatives.										

Rate your effectiveness in the following areas on a scale of 1–10 with 10 being very effective and 1 being ineffective

	Ineffective							Very Effective		
	1	2	3	4	5	6	7	8	9	10
10. When taking on new projects, I commit myself and demonstrate integrity by "walking my talk."										
11. I get team members engaged and committed to a common goal.										
12. I know what I stand for, and the things I do are in line with that commitment.										
13. I keep projects and tasks moving forward.										
14. When momentum is not occurring, I check in with myself or my team to understand what action is needed to get back on track.										
15. I am able to verbalize to team members what the next action is.										
16. I am able to hold myself accountable.										
17. I am able to hold others accountable.										
18. I engage in conversations with others about the specific goals and expectations they are focused on.										
19. When conflict arises, I have a conversation to address it in a timely, calm, and constructive fashion.										
20. I do not fester in anger, bitterness, or resentment.										
21. I am comfortable talking through differences in opinion and observations in order to resolve an issue.										

Rate your effectiveness in the following areas on a scale of 1–10 with 10 being very effective and 1 being ineffective										
	Ineffective							Very Effective		
	1	2	3	4	5	6	7	8	9	10
22. When a situation seems to be in a repeat pattern or if things are not working, I have the conversations necessary to address the issue with the right people.										
23. I catch myself when I am in circular thinking that is preventing me from reaching my goals.										
24. When I am stuck or do not know what to do, I acknowledge it and ask the right people to help me through to the next step.										
25. When a relationship is toxic or one-sided, I am able to have a conversation to disengage and withdraw.										
26. When significant change is needed, I am able to describe the outcomes we are looking for.										
27. I am self-aware and am able to navigate through my emotions surrounding a change situation.										
28. When change has occurred, I am able to have a conversation to initiate or deal with the change.										
29. When I sense a change is on the horizon, I am able to discuss proactively what items need to be considered in light of that future change.										
30. I include other people appropriately so that they understand what is expected of them before, during, and after change initiatives.										

Rate your effectiveness in the following areas on a scale of 1–10 with 10 being very effective and 1 being ineffective

	Ineffective						Very Effective			
	1	2	3	4	5	6	7	8	9	10
31. I regularly demonstrate my appreciation to others in ways that are tailored to them as individuals.										
32. When others acknowledge me, I graciously accept their compliments.										
33. I endorse others, and I am also well endorsed.										
34. When a project is ending, I acknowledge the accomplishments.										
35. When moving on from a team or organization, I leave on good terms and do not burn bridges.										
36. When I or someone I know is leaving a team or an organization, I do something to acknowledge that a "chapter" is ending.										

Now that you have rated yourself, let's see which conversations you engage in most and which ones you will want to focus on developing.

Question #	Conversation Type
1	Connection
2	Connection
3	Connection
4	Creating
5	Creating
6	Creating
7	Structure
8	Structure

Question #	Conversation Type
9	Structure
10	Commitment
11	Commitment
12	Commitment
13	Action
14	Action, Accountability
15	Action, Accountability
16	Accountability
17	Conflict Resolution
18	Breakdown
19	Breakdown
20	Breakdown
21	Withdrawal and Disengage
22	Withdrawal and Disengage
23	Withdrawal and Disengage
24	Change
25	Change
26	Change
27	Appreciation
28	Appreciation
29	Appreciation
30	Moving On
31	Moving On
32	Moving On

The 12 Conversations

Here is a brief look at each of the conversation types.

Conversation for Connection

Connecting with others happens when we slow down enough to be in the present and really listen to one another. Rapport building requires listening now. Can you be here now? Powerful listening causes trust to grow.

Conversation for Creating New Possibilities

The first steps in Conversations for Creating New Possibilities are knowing what we want to create and letting ourselves dream. Conversations can also be the triggers to professional development. Sometimes the questions a manager or colleague asks help us to understand a situation better. We begin to see what is possible.

Conversation for Structure

When we know what we want to create, the next step is to devise a plan. The steps in our plan might only emerge one or several at a time. Nevertheless, we build our plans with the steps as we become aware of them. Maintaining forward movement is vital for long-term success.

Conversation for Commitment

Once a plan and supporting structure are in place and we've identified action steps, we can step back and ask, "Who will execute each step?" We identify potential candidates and then seek their commitment to take the action that produces the result that corresponds with each identified task. The commitments we make to ourselves about *who we want to be* are the most fundamental commitments we will make.

Conversation for Action

Once you know what you want to create, that naturally leads to a conversation about action. What do you want to DO? What actions will make your professional dreams and goals come alive? We've all seen people get stuck in a project because they do not know what to do next. Why the quandary? They're not asking themselves the right questions.

Conversation for Accountability

After a Conversation for Commitment has occurred and the expectations are clear, being accountable for engaging in what you want to do is a sign of respect. Sometimes people need to be guided into creating a better outcome.

Conversation for Conflict Resolution

Many people do not allow themselves to recognize conflicts in their work relationships because they simply do not know how to identify and resolve them. They sweep them under the carpet or wear blinders as a symptom of feeling fear. Some people experience fear when the smell of conflict wafts through a conversation that doesn't offer the requisite safety. Others may overuse this conversation type and not be aware they are doing so.

Conversation for Breakdown

Anger indicates that something or someone has crossed one of our boundaries and is a signal that we need to address the issue. Asking for what we want might clear up the breakdown. Whenever something is not working or we find ourselves oscillating, that is a breakdown. Acknowledging the breakdown is vital so that we can move forward.

Conversation for Withdrawal and Disengagement

It is unrealistic to think that all work relationships will be enjoyable or friendly forever, and not all relationships end on a healthy, happy note. Sometimes we realize it is time to end a relationship, but the other person does not. Often it is best to end a tenuous connection so that we can invest our time in relationships that *are* professionally meaningful and enjoyable.

Conversation for Change

Your ability to change the direction of an individual, a team, or an organization occurs through Conversations for Change. When you need to make change happen, are you competent at guiding the conversations that are necessary? You can change the conversation in the office, at association meetings, at board meetings, and with peers who seem to have gone off track.

Conversation for Appreciation

Being able to create a meaningful conversation that acknowledges and triggers feelings of appreciation is vital to building momentum in professional relationships. Think of the last time you felt really appreciated at work. What caused you to feel this way? Undoubtedly someone showed appreciation to you using language that works best for you. Affirming others is an important conversation to build relationships and momentum.

Conversation for Moving On

Chances are, you have met hundreds or thousands of people in your lifetime, but you maintain close professional relationships with only a few. You create Conversations for Moving On when moving from a community or transferring or retiring from a company. One day you might reconnect, but for now you have closure, with no expectation of communicating again soon.

In the following chapters, we will delve into each conversation type extensively. The first type we will explore in the next chapter is the Conversation for Connection. Whenever we are meeting someone for the first time, interviewing for a project opportunity, or introducing ourselves to a new team, we need to create a meaningful Conversation for Connection.

CHAPTER 5

Conversation for Connection

A Conversation for Connection is the first step in building a relationship that leads to working together to accomplish meaningful results. It enables people to understand one another's preferred communication style. While it may sound initially like small talk, this conversation is in fact very important in helping us get to know each other. We can observe how others pace themselves, gesture, ask questions, listen, enunciate, and maintain eye contact. This gives us clues to their preferred communication style. We can listen for the types of things the other person wants to talk about, which gives us clues to their values and motivators. It also helps us to notice when changes occur in any of these areas later as the conversation goes deeper.

Use this conversation when:

- Meeting new peers, employees, bosses, leaders, colleagues, and team members
- Attending a conference or company meeting
- Interviewing for a project or job or working with a new customer
- Attempting to build a solid foundation of rapport and safety

- Improving or deepening an existing relationship by checking in and sharing news about yourself
- Networking

All about Connection

Recently, I met with a new client, Jason, for our first meeting. The purpose of our meeting was for me to get to know him—who he is today and what he is working on now. A year ago, Jason's organization changed dramatically, and he started working for a new boss. He talked about that for more than an hour, and at least a dozen times he referenced situations that happened over a year ago. Despite my attempts to bring him back to today, to what he was doing now and what his goals were for the next six months, all he could talk about was the way it used to be. He was stuck and didn't even know it. He did not know how to be here now.

I finally asked, "Jason, can you be here now?" He looked at me oddly and said, "I am here now." He was unaware of how much he was living in the past and thus unable to make a connection to today. I said, "You seem to be living in the events and conversations that happened a year ago so I am going to challenge you in the next 30 minutes to stay here, in the present, in this conversation now. Do you think you can do that?" Five minutes later he was laughing at himself because he caught his conversation again returning to last year and all the feelings that it evoked.

Being here now enables a current and authentic connection to occur with the other person. Deep listening can occur only when we are in the present moment. Connecting with others requires that we are first present to what is happening now.

Rapport Building Requires Listening

If we are addicted to the past, being here now requires focus and attention. If we are overly fixated on the future, we are overfocused on what we are planning for next month or next year instead of being in the present and building from this moment.

The easiest way to bring yourself into the present is to breathe deeply and feel the breath you are taking in at this moment. Slow your thinking down. Feel your heart beating now. If you can do that during conversations, you will help yourself to be present. When we are in the now, amazing things happen. We can begin to flow in the path of least resistance; in other words, less effort is required for us to succeed in a conversation because we are paying attention to connecting now. We focus our intention on this moment and this conversation.

Fortunately, we do not have to ask in-depth or pointed questions to create meaningful, rapport-building conversations. Being present and listening creates more intimacy than asking repeated, probing questions that control the direction of the conversation. A manager will do wonders for building rapport and trust by asking open-ended questions such as "How's your project going?," by listening to and looking the employee in the eye as she responds, and, when the employee is finished speaking, by summarizing what she said.

One executive I coached was given this feedback in a 360 debrief session: "She rarely listens because she usually has a series of questions she wants answered. There is no room for the conversation to go any way but her way." To change this perception and experience for her employees, I advised the executive to drop by her employees' offices from time to time, simply ask how they are doing, and then listen. Such listening requires being fully present, maintaining eye contact for at least three to four seconds at a time (without darting your eyes), mentally summarizing what you are hearing, and then asking questions about what has been said. It will take several of these encounters for employees to trust that this executive is truly ready to listen in a way that allows growth to emerge in their conversations. This kind of powerful listening causes trust to grow and can make a huge difference in how one is perceived.

Connecting with People You Have Known a Long Time

Like many of us, you've probably known some people for many years. Think about some of these relationships: are any of them stuck in the place they were years ago, and now you really don't know who that person is today? In this situation, creating a new Conversation for Connection necessitates concentration and focus. Ask questions as if you were meeting for the first time, such as "Tell me about what is most important to you? What are you enjoying lately? What hobbies have you taken up? Or perhaps, How do you think your career came to be where it is now?"

Authentically discuss what is true now for yourself too. You might say something like "We worked closely together several years ago, and I realize I do not know much about who you are today! It is refreshing to reconnect with you." Amazing things may unfold. If someone has grown and changed and it seems they've "forgotten" to tell you, then you've probably grown and changed in that time too. The best thing you can do is catch up with each other so you're both current.

Making New Connections

I had an experience of serendipity by being present in the moment and listening to my instincts. I was at a business meeting in a city hours from my normal routine, and as is usually the case, I was feeling hopeful. When I arrived, I had a strong desire to sit in a particular area, and so I followed that nudge and requested the table I wanted. After being seated and ordering my meal, I again sensed the kind of nudge that we only notice when we are in the present moment; it prompted me to think, "Ask the waitress where she goes to school." I did so and discovered she was attending the same university I attended. We then proceeded to have a delightful Conversation for Connection in which she told me she was studying in *my* field. She was looking for an internship in the city where I now work. I happen to know someone who was looking for someone like her. I gave her my card and told her I could connect her to someone she'd enjoy meeting. She is now working for that company as a result of the Conversation for Connection we had. Serendipity like this happens when you stay in the moment.

If you're just getting to know a business acquaintance, I've found meeting for coffee, tea, or lunch enables a conversation to break away from the distractions and business of the office. Have you noticed this too? Are you using this awareness when you schedule meetings to get to know new people better? Long, slow dinners also contribute to Conversations for Connection, as Keith Ferrazzi points out in *Who's Got Your Back*. Keith says this is one of the best ways of deepening a relationship. During a long, slow dinner people stop watching the clock, let down their defenses, and look beyond preconceptions and emotional baggage so they can seek out shared ideas.

It is easiest to make a connection with people when talking about what is most important to them. Our values are the key to the deepest connections we create. Oprah Winfrey is an example of someone who intentionally connects with people on a values level, going right to the core of what it means to live your best life. You will develop sincere connections with people by being yourself, using your natural communication style, and showing your vulnerability by expressing your feelings in the moment. President Barack Obama's campaign focused on just these elements as he and his supporters created connections across generations, organizations, and states. Executive recruiters are also well known for creating relationships with many people across industries, professions, and organizations. LinkedIn, a professional networking Web site, is the primary tool that professional businesspeople use to share who they are and make new connections online.

Dan Nye, a board member at Constant Contact and the former CEO of LinkedIn, shared with me his perspective on how to create just such a Conversation for Connection. "When you want to meet someone you have not met before, contact them through a mutual friend and help them understand why it's in *their* best interest to meet with *you*. Don't come on too strong. Doing so will only turn off the person you are trying to reach and hurt your relationship with the person making the intro-duction. Also, don't only ask for assistance. Be sure to give back too. If you take the time to do valuable things for others, they in turn will do things for you."

Dan went on to say, when you lead a meeting to create a Conversation for Connection with the attendees, "Start by set-ting the stage. At the beginning of every meeting, state the objective of the meeting, provide a brief summary of relevant information, and clarify the desired outcome. By setting the stage well, you set the tone, confirm you have the right people involved to achieve the desired goal, and obtain focus from par-ticipants. Often what is missing when people trip up is that they don't do the necessary prework for the meeting, don't set the stage correctly, don't manage the meeting efficiently, don't sum-marize the decisions, conclusions, and next steps properly, or don't document the results immediately afterward."

Conversations Done Right

Here are some examples of how it sounds when a Conversation for Connection goes well.

Jean and Bob

This is the story of Jean and Bob, who worked in different areas of a bank. In a large bank with a central processing area for counting and distributing money to its branches, the Cash Pro-cessing department is the area in which the money is handled. This department has high security and is usually very busy throughout the day. Cleaning and Janitorial Services is another department in the bank. At this particular bank, the two depart-ments were not working well together because the members of the cleaning staff wanted to show up to clean the Cash Process-ing department whenever it fit their busy schedule. The Cash Processing staff did not have the ability to randomly let the cleaning staff into the high-security area in which money was constantly being counted. Tensions were high between the supervisors of each group. They did not have a connection and, as a result, butted heads for several months.

The supervisor of the Cash Processing department, Jean, attended the When the Conversation Changes workshop (www. WhentheConversationChanges.com). During the workshop, Jean realized that she had no safe conversation connection with the other supervisor, Bob. They were an automatic "no" to each other because no one was listening. Jean decided she would connect with Bob in a new way. She considered his preferred communication style and motivators and imagined what he might be feeling. She thought about how best to interact with him to change their existing conversation.

Jean invited Bob to have a cup of coffee in the company café. She said, "Bob, I'd really like to understand what your needs are. I've been feeling uncomfortable about this conflict between our departments. I'm wondering if we can get to know each other better so we can understand what each other's real needs are."

Then, she listened.

Jean really listened while maintaining eye contact and nodding her head in acknowledgment. She summarized what she heard Bob say. She asked a few questions for clarity about his point of view, and she kept eye contact with Bob even though others walked by them at the table. She asked several more questions in order to determine Bob's preferred communication style and understand what was expected of his department. Next she paused to see if he wanted to add anything else. Then Jean shared her thoughts, her feelings, and the areas in which she believed the differences in their needs were getting in the way. She suggested they both think about what could be done and sleep on it for a few days. She realized Bob was not someone who liked to make quick decisions, even though that was her personal preference.

When they met two days later, it was clear that they each cared about coming up with a solution that worked for both departments. Both Jean and Bob later said that meeting over coffee, away from their offices, made a big difference in their ability to change the conversational dynamics. For the first time, real listening was occurring on both sides of the table. They were able to move beyond blame and finger-pointing to explore real solutions. From there, they moved into a Conversation for Creating New Possibilities, as we will discuss in Chapter 6.

Dianne

I had a coaching client, Dianne, who was putting together a presentation introducing herself to 80 people in the new department where she is now a vice president. As we helped her prepare the content for her presentation, I told her that, typically, when I do a presentation of vital importance (such as the one she was giving to the whole department), I will have an *informal* talk in advance with 5 to 10 people who will be in the audience at the time of the presentation. I gently and confidently probe for information with statements and questions like these:

- I want to make sure I am aligned with the values and culture of the organization in my presentation and delivery. How would you describe the values and the culture?
- I also want to understand the needs of the audience and their predominant communication style. What do you notice about the communication styles of the members of this department?
- Because I value your opinion, would you be willing to tell me what you believe is needed for a successful presentation with this group?

These individual, pre-presentation conversations help you to connect to your larger audience by giving you their language, recent examples, and questions they have about you or your topic. Weaving in that you spoke to several members of the audience prior to the presentation builds rapport with the whole audience, showing you cared enough to learn about them before taking the stage.

If I were introducing myself to a new team or group of employees, I might give a survey before the presentation asking everyone who will attend questions like "What do you want to know about my role and priorities? What do you want me to know about you and the organization?" This enables you to say in your presentation, "I'm going to answer the questions you asked . . ."

No matter what type of presentation you are delivering, having a behind-the-scenes, one-on-one conversation with 5 to 10 people (even if just by phone) will also prove useful before meeting with the whole group. These conversations aren't just to get information; they also help the people you are engaging with realize that you value their input, and they will feel like they helped you to succeed. They will be more invested in your success because they had this private, confidential conversation with you. This is an influence strategy to help you build meaningful relationship connections.

The key is for you to be confident in yourself while asking the questions. Keep in mind you are listening for cultural information, and saying or creating the impression that you feel up to the challenge. The time and energy you spend planning and preparing for this will result in a better presentation as well as stronger relationships with the people you consulted with beforehand. By using these ideas, Dianne was able to build rapport with the new global department she recently joined. She met all the members of the department, was able to help them understand her role, and set realistic expectations. This paved the way for her to be successful in this new organization.

Nancy

Nancy is a proud member of the Forum of Executive Women. She recently met several new members of this organization at a restaurant for dinner, and she found it easy to spark Conversations for Connection. No one needed to say, "We are in a Conversation for Connection." Rather, Nancy asked questions and shared information about herself that provided interesting details for others to prompt more conversation. This is what the beginning of the conversation sounded like:

Nancy: *Hi Pat, I'm excited to meet you.*

Pat: *I've heard such good things about this group that I wanted to come see for myself, why the buzz? How long have you been a member?*

Nancy: *Four years. I think you'll find many ways to become active and meet people. What are you interested in participating in?*

Pat: *I have been exploring the ways in which . . .*

Naturally, other people who were at the table couldn't help but jump into the discussion. This conversation easily builds on itself as additional people join the dinner table. Two hours later, they had shared their business goals, challenges, and vacation dreams for next year. A connection was made. People take for granted sometimes the fact that it's easy to make new business connections just by chatting with the people you encounter informally. Never be too shy to start a Conversation for Connection.

Silvia

Silvia read a book that she enjoyed. Her respect for the author and the topic caused Silvia to think about whether it might be possible to get to know the author personally. She finally decided to write to the well-known author and share why the book had such a strong impact on her. She sent a handwritten letter on beautiful stationery. To her surprise, the author wrote back and suggested that the next time Silvia was in New York City, they could get together for coffee. Silvia jumped at this opportunity and created a reason to go to New York. During their first in-person meeting, Silvia asked questions, shared more details about why the book was relevant to her, and listened as the author talked about a new book she was considering writing. They became friends who regularly e-mail back and forth sharing ideas. This Conversation for Connection created a meaningful professional relationship that has inspired both women over many years.

While not every professional will turn out to be as approachable, Dr. Jeff Silber shared this example of a Conversation for Connection:

Many years ago, I was a faculty member at a university hospital. I was interviewing one of the flood of residency applicants for the coming year. I'd noticed that he was getting a DO rather than an MD. With a friendly smile, I asked him, "So tell me, what is a DO, someone who couldn't get into medical school?" The key was that I did not ask in a derogatory way or with a condescending tone of voice. I asked as an entrée to why he chose to do what he did. We had a conversation about osteopathy, homeopathy, and chiropractic that taught me some things. He selected our hospital and became one of our best-ever chief residents. He told me years later that he'd always remembered and appreciated our first conversation because of the candor in approaching what is often a subverted and misunderstood topic, as well as the openness in showing true interest in and accepting his answers. We are still friends today. It started with one Conversation for Connection.

Phrases and Questions to Start a Conversation

Here are some ways to get your Conversation for Connection started:

- "Bob Jones suggested we connect with each other, and I wanted to reach out to you to see if we might be able to have a cup of coffee together sometime since he thought we'd enjoy meeting each other."
- "How did you come to work at this organization?"
- "What are you passionate about?"
- "How did you meet Bob?"
- "I checked out your LinkedIn profile and noticed that we both know Sara Smith. How did you meet her?"
- "I understand you have extensive experience in . . . , and I'd love to hear about it."
- "Where is your accent from?"
- "I noticed in the newspaper this morning . . ."
- "What are some of the current trends you are seeing in your work? How are you dealing with those trends?"

- "What did you enjoy studying in school, and have you been using that in your work?"
- "What are some of your favorite work experiences?"
- "What caused you to come to this meeting/conference/company?"
- "What types of projects are you currently working on?"
- "How did you get into your line of work? This association?"
- "Do you use LinkedIn or Facebook? What has been your experience with it?"
- "What do you do when you are not attending the XYZ meeting or working for this organization?"
- "What's new with you since we saw each other last?"
- "How is your project going?"
- "What's on your mind?"
- "You seem excited. What's happening?"
- "I am doing research about how project managers approach challenges in their work, and I know you have extensive expertise in working with project managers. Would you be willing to talk with me about this to share your experience?"

Other ways to create meaningful conversations include:

- Share your own good news.
- Share something you learned that is interesting or useful.
- Tell a story that amused you.
- Mention a new product you recently tried, and share what happened.
- Talk about a trend you have observed, and ask if the other person has noticed this too.

Mistakes in Conversation

The biggest mistake professionals make in the workplace related to this type of conversation is that either they do not have them at all or they rush through them. They jump over them and dive into the work at hand. This is a mistake, because if we do not understand the other person's workplace motivators and communication-style preferences, we can easily create gaps in understanding. It is easy to miss nuances and details that can throw us off course later on. When this conversation is not in place, you miss out on the opportunity to make better connections in order to improve your professional and personal relationships.

When There's No Conversation

The following problems can result when the Conversation for Connection is missing:

- We have few new relationships.
- We assume that we already know the other person well enough and that nothing new or important is going on in his or her life.
- Relationships become all business, and the emotional connection that causes inspiration and loyalty either never forms or falls apart.
- Leaders who do not build connections with their team may seem like they are using positional power, and they may be undermined by their team.
- We may not have the opportunity to make a "fit" into a new organization, department, or culture.

Final Words

Conversations for Connection require listening by being fully present; maintaining eye contact, summarizing what you are hearing, and then asking questions about what has been said. Deep listening builds trust and safety in relationships.

When Conversations for Connection are missing, you lose out on opportunities to make deeper connections that will improve your professional and personal relationships and opportunities.

An influence strategy focused on building meaningful relation-ships and new connections will pay off with an expanded net-work, people to bounce ideas around with, and new opportunities. Be confident in your ability to create Conversations for Connec-tion by practicing this conversation with someone new each day. Challenge yourself to people-read someone, exploring what that person's preferred communication style is and what workplace motivators drive him or her to achieve.

Conversation for Creating New Possibilities

Knowing what we want to create and letting ourselves dream is the first step in Conversations for Creating New Possibilities. People who have made meaningful contributions have allowed themselves to think in new ways about what could be. Product innovations, new organization structures, and new positions began with a Conversation for Creating New Possibilities.

Use this conversation when:

- Brainstorming new ideas
- Proposing a new idea or solution for a problem
- Uncovering ideas from peers and team members
- Trying to solve a problem that needs a new solution that is not currently clear to you

All about Creating New Possibilities

Milton S. Hershey opened Hershey Park in 1907 in Hershey, Pennsylvania. He created this amusement park because he wanted to provide a place for his employees to take their families for fun on the weekends. Today, in the central Pennsylvania area, Hershey Park is still a popular family destination that enables people from all over to appreciate his creation.

Disneyland opened in 1955 in Anaheim, California, and Disney World opened in Orlando, Florida, in 1971. These parks were founded by Walt Disney in his effort to create the best amusement parks for families to have fun. To keep the parks growing, he also set a goal that each year a new attraction would be built at each park. This goal, and the ongoing conversation focused on keeping this spirit of imagination alive, set the Disney parks apart from the rest. They regularly innovate based on Conversations for Creating New Possibilities.

A new theme park attraction may not be what your office needs right now, but in order to create new possibilities for your company, someone needs to do what Walt Disney did and play a leadership role inviting new possibilities to be explored. So, verbally put a stake in the ground that announces you are ready for new ideas. Or, another example, unequivocally say that you and your team members, are committed to excellent service and are willing to explore new ways of delivering outstanding customer experiences. These openings will encourage ideas that will lead to innovation and growth.

Having the spirit of an adventurer or an explorer enables us to see in new ways. The feeling of hope is often associated with being able to see new possibilities. Have you noticed when you feel hopeful, that's when an avalanche of new ideas tends to show up? Sometimes to kick-start a discussion for new possibilities, I encourage people to recall the last time they felt really hopeful about something and to describe it in detail. This will trigger the feeling of hope to show up again now as we begin the exploration.

In *The Magic of Thinking Big,* author David Schwartz says, "Believe Big. The size of your success is determined by the size of your belief. Think little goals and expect little achievements. Think big goals and win big success. Remember this, too. Big ideas and big plans are often easier—certainly no more difficult—than small ideas and small plans." He is encouraging us to think in new ways, to innovate and explore, creating new possibilities.

Imagination is everything.
It is a preview of life's coming attractions.
—Albert Einstein

When we are not stuck, we want to create and grow, using our imagination to dream up new adventures for ourselves and others. Conversations can trigger new personal and professional development. Sometimes questions from a manager or colleague can help us better understand a situation or ourselves, and then we begin to see new possibilities. What do you want to create? Can you list 100 opportunities, things, experiences, conversations, companies you'd like to work with, or assignments you want? This gets your creative juices flowing. Give it a try.

If you cannot answer these questions, you may be stuck. Sometimes people create their own glass ceilings to growth by limiting their options. If you said, "I could list 20 opportunities I'd like to create for myself, but 100 is too many," then you are creating your own glass ceiling limiting what you believe is possible for you. A breakthrough occurs for people when they actually do this activity, because it pushes them through their own thinking barriers. New possibilities do not have to be grand or even expensive. Something as simple as wanting to meet all the people in your sales department, including the new director, or wanting to explore how to use a new technology may be on your list.

If you do feel stuck, and you're open to receiving help in getting unstuck, it is best to ask for it. Call a boss or a peer, and let that person know you would like help getting unstuck. Have the person ask questions about what you want to create or about whatever project you're working on so you can uncover what's going on. Some of us need to verbalize our thinking so we are aware of what we want. Others need private time to mull over these questions alone to uncover what their own answers are.

Doing so will open the door to a healthy conversation with the potential for growth and discovery, and *that's* having a Conversation for Creating New Possibilities.

These are conversations for growth and new possibilities, and they need breathing room. We do not have to be in conversation every moment we are together, especially if we are spending more than a few hours together. I can't process an ongoing stream of talk. It makes me feel exhausted, and even when given a little quiet time to check in with myself, I can't think clearly. Business meetings that have a break every 45 to 65 minutes are more effective for creating new ideas than those that go on for hours. Breaks provide time to create new thinking.

Our questions can be an invitation for new possibilities if we frame them properly. Most people do not ask colleagues for a tour of their home and say, "Where do you keep your junk? Will you please show me your dirty clothes basket?" While we might be close enough to ask for help on organizing the file system or giving tips on stain removal for a shirt we dripped soup on at lunch, we probably don't want colleagues probing into that area without invitation. Therefore, if managers show up to a meeting and start asking each other how are things going with their worst employees, or what's happening with a difficult situation they discussed last week, they are demanding we start with our dirty laundry, and that's not likely to create space for safety and new thinking.

Similarly, we don't want to hang out with people who go to get their dirty laundry each time they see us. This sounds like "Hey, let me tell you about this awful thing that happened to me with my boss. You will not believe what a jerk he is and how stupidly my peer acted." Retelling a pointless tale of mistakes, missed client opportunities, dumb comments in a meeting, misfiled files, or bad service only creates bad feelings. Let's say, "ENOUGH." Change the conversation. Focus on something you want to create.

When someone continues to ask questions about what other
people are doing or questions that trigger painful memories,

you should realize that they are lacking drama in their own life or are hoping to create some in yours. Either that or they are in some subconscious pain of their own and want you to mirror that. I refer to such conversations as "Dirty Laundry Conversations," and these will not help at all if your goal is to create new possibilities.

You do not have to offer drama or be the mirror for someone when it does not support your intentions for yourself, your team, or your business. Dirty Laundry Conversations are a bad habit of human communication, and second nature for many of us. Becoming aware of this pattern helps us create better conversations in the office, at conferences, during board meetings, and with our bosses. Change the conversation by asking, "What do you want to create next?"

Letting Go to Grow

In the past, I might've gotten stuck in a painful question that a peer asked at work, and I might've spent hours or days struggling with it, talking it over, and thinking it was purposeful. Have you ever spent time silently fuming? This is emotionally draining and does not produce anything worthwhile for anyone. Now I'm free. I know I can breathe it out and deeply let it go. You've got to be in the moment, aware of what you're feeling, and willing to engage in purposeful conversation that builds on what you want to create next. Staying in the moment enables continued growth and new possibilities.

There's also a correlation between emotional junk stored in the body and physical junk stored in an office or all over the desk and conference table. When there is too much junk cluttering your space or emotions, growth and new creation cannot occur. When you let go of something on one level, it has an impact on the other. A client of mine, Andy, noticed a correlation between holding a grudge because of a comment that a coworker made and not being able to be fully present with that coworker in later conversations. When Andy brought up the issue that was causing him to hold onto emotional junk and worked through it with the coworker, there was a new clearing in their communication with each other. Metaphorically, the shelf had been cleared, and now new topics could emerge for discussion. Growth emerged as a result of simply letting go and creating space.

A colleague of mine is looking for a new job. His workspace is cluttered and covered with mail and piles of paper. Every space in his office is occupied, and there is no room for anything new. This same correlation exists between his cluttered office and the lack of new job opportunities that show up for him. His lack of focus shows up clearly in both areas. There is no space for these new opportunities to appear. To make space for what I want, I have to let go of what I do not want. I shared with this colleague that how we approach our space is often representative of how we approach conversations. Clutter is a sign that we are not making decisions about what we need and want to do. When there is clutter in your space, you may also lack intention about the conversations you are creating.

I told a professional colleague about the Japanese tradition of having an empty shelf in the office closet so there is always room. I've found that having empty shelves in my office and bookcases provides a little room to breathe new life into my surroundings and reminds me to be open to new possibilities. When I buy a new book, I give an old one to the newest hire on the team. When I open a new client file, I check to see if there is an outdated one that needs to be purged. This habit creates a feeling of abundance and satisfaction with what I already have. It builds the muscle of intention in what I am doing, which is vital to being conscious about what type of conversation I am creating.

This concept sparked a lightbulb moment for another peer of mine. She said, "I can't have the type of conversations I want to experience with some of the people currently on my team. I've tried everything possible for a few years, and I gave up, but didn't do anything to change the situation. There are just too many ill feelings cluttering up our conversation. I really want a different type of team environment, but to get it I'm going to have to clear the shelf and create different conversations." She went back to her office and literally cleaned out her files and bookshelves and physically made space for something new. She also began to focus on creating the type of conversations that were most meaningful to her. Less than a year later she was in a new role with a new team, feeling much better about her ability to connect in meaningful ways that enable growth. She also had empty space on her shelves as a reminder to be open to new possibilities.

Creating New Possibilities by Sharing Connections

A professional mentor of mine, Marilyn, has a diverse group of colleagues and clients, some much younger or older than she is. She deliberately built professional relationships with people who were not in her age range. I was a college student when she was well into her career, and we became colleagues because she initiated the conversation.

As I got to know the people in her network, I realized she has several people that she talks with regularly whose ages are all over the place. I also noticed a common theme. Marilyn values seeking truth and wisdom and sharing knowledge in practical ways. Her top values are *theoretical* and *utilitarian*. She has collected kindred spirits who also read and share books focused on useful information, and she surrounds herself with people who have these traits in common. It is the glue that has caused momentum in dozens of her relationships. Her relationships with these people have withstood many different types of changes. Some of them have changed companies, professions, and associations; however, they still stay in an ongoing conversation with each other.

When we deliberately build relationships based on our values, something amazing happens. We know what other people value and can guide conversations in the direction of what is most meaningful to them. We can make connections for others so that our colleagues and peers enjoy meeting each other

83

because we show them the common theme in their values. We are aware enough to know which people to connect with each other, and our relationships acquire momentum.

I serve on the board of a professional association, and I recently proposed a regular book discussion group so that we could get to know each other better by discussing business books of interest to us. One of the members of this group, John, did this brilliantly by holding the discussion in his office and choosing a book that he really enjoyed reading. The group was invited to read *Executive Presence: The Art of Communicating Respect Like a CEO* by Harrison Monarth. The meeting was a huge success, and we were each able to meet more like-minded people as a result.

I do the same when I host executive briefings for my clients, dinners for colleagues, or forums to discuss topics of interest with a mix of people I know. I invite people who I know would enjoy something based on common values. Sharing colleagues becomes an act of service, as I am appreciating others by connecting them with people they will enjoy meeting. *New conversations and, hence, new relationships and possibilities emerge.* I love asking myself this question: "How are you helping the people you know by connecting them to others with similar values?"

In *Never Eat Alone*, Keith Ferrazzi says, "Until you become as willing to ask for help as you are to give it, you are only working half the equation. That's what I mean by connecting. It's a constant process of giving and receiving—of asking for and offering help. By putting people in contact with one another, by giving your time and expertise and sharing them freely, the pie gets bigger for everyone."

The Possibility of Transformation

Having a Conversation for Creating New Possibilities means opening yourself up to the many ways you can transform your life and work, as well as the experience of those who share your life. If you're uncertain what to focus such a conversation on, ask yourself, "What aspects of my life do I want to create, develop, or improve?" Triggers for this line of thinking might include:

- Body and health
- Mind and thinking
- Relationships
- Emotional intelligence
- Spiritual life
- Technological skill
- Environment and space
- Education and learning
- Family
- Friends
- Work and career
- Charities
- Hobbies and interests

Businesses are transformed by having a group of people focus their conversations on a specific theme for 30, 60, or 90 days, a concept that we will explore in more detail in Chapter 10. A daily or weekly conversation that focuses on the specific goal or outcome keeps the momentum going. A new manager, Ruth, and her team decided to do a five-minute check-in each morning in which they would have one of the team members read out loud the team's 90-day goals. They rotated who read the goals each morning. Each of Ruth's team members commented on how powerful this was in keeping them focused and aligned on the goals they agreed to. By doing this each morning, they changed the conversation that began their day. They met their new goals faster than they anticipated and claimed it was because they were focused together on making it happen. This team decided to keep the momentum going by setting a new norm and making the first conversation of the day focused on goals.

Creating New Possibilities by Staying Connected

Building healthy, long-lasting relationships requires staying connected and following up in meaningful ways. There have been times when I've undergone some kind of change and neglected to tell others about my development. Keeping others updated works to your advantage. A company blog, a newsletter, a regular coffee date, a long walk, a phone conversation—all these can be useful new possibilities for maintaining business relationships.

For the people who are important to us, we need to create regular idea exchanges for staying connected, especially when we know changes are coming. Creating a regular conversation to explore possibilities together makes this happen. Moving across the country doesn't mean we have to lose important business connections. Telecommuting from home doesn't mean we have to lose valuable relationships with colleagues. We just have to decide what follow-up will work best for us to stay connected and continue exploring together.

Elizabeth has been a mentor of mine for over 20 years. She and I have a commitment to regularly be in conversation, sharing and exploring our newest learning with each other. As part of that commitment, we make plans to talk weekly and get together at conferences, even though we live in different states. Similarly, I stay connected with clients I have not seen recently by having a quarterly check-in or inviting them to an executive briefing meeting to explore a new idea or topic together.

Martin Luther King, Jr., Nelson Mandela, Thomas Edison, Steven Hawking, Steve Jobs, and Bill Gates are individuals who clearly created Conversations for New Possibilities first on an individual level and then on a global level. They kept these conversations alive with their audience. They explored and created new possibilities that affect our present everyday working environment. Apple, Google, QVC, the Future Search Network, Saint Jude Children's Research Hospital, and Penn Medical Researchers are examples of organizations that are known for creating new possibilities and keeping the connection going so ongoing growth occurs.

Conversations Done Right

Here are some examples of how it sounds when a Conversation for Creating New Possibilities goes well.

Myra

Myra is the leader of a large team within an organization that had been in existence for over a hundred years. Myra runs the sales organization that is responsible for bringing in new subscribers to an expensive service. She had an emerging awareness that there wasn't much diversity represented in the group. She realized that the members of the group were all within 10 years of the same age, had similar educational backgrounds, had the same color of skin, and had a similar religious background. For this organization to grow and perhaps even stay alive, Myra knew it would be important for the group to become more aware of the impact of diversity. She approached one of her colleagues, Joe, who she knew understood the value of listening to enable people to process their thinking. She initiated a Conversation for Creating New Possibilities with him about how she wanted to deal with this issue. How could her team best sell to emerging markets and people who were very different from the team members?

During the conversation with Joe, she decided she wanted individuals on the team both to create opportunities that would broaden their level of experience and to seek out diverse candidates to work for the organization in the future. To make this happen, Myra would have to get her team members engaged in this possibility with her. She invited her senior managers to attend a meeting with the agenda focused on asking them to think about ways they could raise awareness about new ideas regarding diversity on the team and in the organization. During this two-hour meeting they brainstormed a list of ways they could expand their awareness and become more inclusive of various types: age, educational background, race, sexual orientation, religious background, and gender.

Together they generated over a dozen possibilities—some much better than others—but there was no evaluation of the ideas during the meeting. All were listed on the large whiteboard equally. At the end of the meeting they were asked to select several of the ideas that they thought would make the most meaningful difference. They identified the top four ideas as key priorities they could each focus on individually. As a member of the senior team, each meeting attendee had employees who reported to them, so someone suggested including the whole organization in this Conversation for New Possibilities. They already had a meeting scheduled for the whole department in two months, so together they agreed to focus two hours during that meeting discussing these ideas.

When they brought the large group together, one of the senior leaders shared that the team had a commitment to raise awareness about the importance of diversity, as the organization wanted to grow and continue to improve its global market position. He shared all the ideas that the senior team brainstormed and asked the rest of the staff to add onto the possibilities. They brainstormed in small groups for 30 minutes and came up with additional possibilities. This got the whole group engaged in the conversation together. After the brainstorming, they sorted the ideas into three buckets:

1. Easy to implement (low-hanging fruit that will produce good results)
2. Difficult to implement (but would clearly pay off with long-term results)
3. Difficult to implement (and may not produce results)

Next, they asked which ideas team members had the most energy for taking on. This Conversation for New Possibilities raised awareness and pointed the way for this team to focus together on specific actions that they could take to increase diversity in their organization. This created many new conversations, all inspired by Myra's initial conversation with herself about creating possibilities.

Karen

Karen, the director of a large team, was not holding regular all-staff meetings with her department. This caused a lot of gossip, and the rumor mill was running wild with speculation, simply because she had not created a way for people to ask her directly about what was on their minds.

We put in place a monthly town hall meeting that she facilitated for the whole team. In these meetings, she and the managers on her team began by updating everyone on news and current events that impacted the department and the company. Then they had an open forum, asking questions like "What is working well that you want to continue?" "What would you like to see more of?" "What would you like less of?" "What are the most important priorities from your perspective?" Karen encouraged all the employees to ask questions and share ideas and suggestions. Part of the meeting specifically focused on generating new ideas, new ways to approach the business. These meetings changed the attitude and dynamics of the department, and enabled everyone to experience the power that comes from being able to create new possibilities together as a collaborative team.

Phrases and Questions to Start a Conversation

Here are some ways to get your Conversation for Creating New Possibilities started:

- "What would you like to create?"
- "I have an idea I'd like you to consider, and I'd be open to hearing your ideas too."
- "What are the options? Can we come up with three or more options that we had not considered before?"
- "If we waved a magic wand and the problem was solved, how would we know? What would be different?"
- "What ideas or suggestions do you have about how we should approach this?"
- "Tell me about your goals and objectives. Where do you see things going . . ."
- "If you could be the best at one thing, what would that one thing be?"

89

- "If you knew you would not fail, what would you do?"
- "Imagine that you just won $3 million. What would you do with it?" *(Let yourself play with this question as if it just happened.)*
- "I'd like to increase the number of people who are submitting their ideas so we have maximum user-generated content. What else could we do to invite people to submit their suggestions and ideas?"
- "Let's see if we can come up with 50 ideas in the next 10 minutes. No idea is too trivial or out of bounds. We are looking for volume now, and we'll come back and edit them later."
- "Tell me about your thoughts about how to improve or change the situation."
- "What do you think it will take to get there? Are there possibilities we have not yet explored?"
- "Perhaps if we considered this in a new way, we could put our puzzle pieces on the table together and see what we come up with."
- "Can we discuss the possibility of . . . ?"
- "If you could envision the best possible outcome, what would that look like?"
- "If there were no limitations, what resources would you need?"
- "People invented the rules. When you are creating, approach it from the angle that there are no rules, or that the rules can be changed if needed. What rules are holding us back that we could consider revising?"
- "What have you learned from your past that impacts this situation? How can we build on that with new ideas?"
- *With someone who has read this book or attended the seminar:* "I'd like to have a Conversation for Creating New Possibilities. When would be a good time for you to do that?"

Mistakes in Conversation

If you judge an idea as soon as it is put on the table for discussion, it causes others to stop sharing creative ideas. If the whole team isn't participating in a discussion, call on those who have not yet shared their thinking and ask them a question. Listen to what others are saying, and wait a bit to respond. Automatically saying no to someone else's ideas will shut the person down and will likely have a dampening effect on others too. Better to say something like "Let me give that some consideration, and I will get back to you." When you get back to the person by pointing out what you liked about the suggestion before explaining the reason you do not think you should move forward with the idea, the difference in how the person receives the negative news is huge.

Seek shared meaning to ensure that your language means the same thing to each of you. In today's world, it is too easy to get lost in technobabble, acronyms, or jargon and think that we do understand each other when we don't, or vice versa. One way to do this is to confirm your understanding using different words from those in the original proposal.

When There's No Conversation

The following problems can result when the Conversation for Creating New Possibilities is missing:

- No new goals or dreams bubble up.
- We hear or think, "That is not the way we do it around here."
- Creativity and innovation are drained.
- There is a judgmental attitude about new ideas.

Organizations that most creatively incorporate diversity of thinking will reap the rewards of innovation, growth, wealth and progress.
—Joel Barker

Final Words

To make space for what we want, we have to be willing to let go of what we do not want. This habit creates a feeling of abundance and satisfaction that opens new doors. Dirty Laundry Conversations are a bad habit of human conversation, but are unfortunately second nature to many people. Learn to transform them. Becoming aware of this pattern will help you to create better conversations no matter where you are. When you catch yourself in a Dirty Laundry Conversation, stop and shift the focus to a new possibility.

Conversations for Creating New Possibilities are focused on solutions, growth, and opportunity. They need breathing room so they can come alive. Our questions become an invitation for new possibilities if we frame them focused on solutions.

CHAPTER 7

Conversation for Structure

When we know what we want to create, the next step is to create a plan for how to get there. We build our plans with the steps involved as we see them. Sometimes we only see the next step or next two steps, not the whole sequence. That's where a Conversation for Structure comes in. Creating a solid structure and gaining forward movement are key to success. At times we are engaged in creating the steps in the structure, and at other times we are listening to understand what the structure will be and confirming our understanding. Both of these are examples of Conversations for Structure.

Use this conversation when:

- Laying out a project plan and schedule
- Discussing how you will bring your goals alive
- Negotiating the details of how something will be done
- Establishing expectations about what will be happening next
- Ensuring others understand the sequence of actions or events they will be involved in
- Creating a process map outlining the specific steps involved

All about Structure

Sometimes Conversations for Structure sound one-sided because one person may be explaining to others what steps will need to be taken next in order to set expectations correctly. This is what happens when we board a plane and the flight attendant explains the procedures. The whole process helps to create order and common understanding on an airplane. We are free to ask questions to ensure our meaning when the flight attendant is finished. The same thing happens when the team leader stands in front of the team members and describes the next steps that need to be taken in order to meet the team objectives and then asks if there are any questions.

Recently I worked with a leadership team from a large global pharmaceutical company that is committed to developing future leaders. The members of the team knew what they wanted to create—a pipeline of developing leaders. What they were unclear on was how to make their goals a reality. They needed to have a Conversation for Structure. They asked for my ideas about how they could best meet their goals. I proposed a mentoring program and laid out four different types of mentoring programs. Then I provided the specific details of how we would build each of the four different mentoring structures and what the impact would be of choosing each of the four options. They made the decisions that were best for their organization. Then they asked me to structure how mentees would be matched to mentors, which I handled for them as well. This organization is very good at Conversations for Creating New Possibilities. Where the company leaders appear to get stuck is in the Conversation for Structure that needs to follow. They are wise enough to bring in other people to help them move through what does not come naturally to them.

Financial planners, accountants, professional organizers, and medical staff regularly engage in Conversations for Structure. Six Sigma, the Project Management Institute (PMI), Accenture, McKenzie, the IRS, and the Red Cross are organizations that are well known for being able to create meaningful Conversations for Structure.

It is not uncommon for people to set big goals without thinking through how they will bring the goals alive. In fact, this happens regularly in a Conversation for Creating New Possibilities. We need to follow that conversation with a focus on structure for success to occur. One of the places this often happens for individuals is when they set a goal to lose weight and maintain high energy levels. If they do not also create a Conversation for Structure, then the goal does not come to be. Realizing what you can remove from your diet and what you can add to your exercise routine is the first step. The second step might be figuring out how to do so on a day-to-day basis. The third step might be figuring out how to keep yourself in check for the long term. If you have set a similar goal to lose weight but have not seen results, I would propose to you that it may be in part because you have not set up a structure for how to accomplish a goal like "no flour, no sugar." *The 150 Healthiest Foods on Earth,* by Jonny Bowden, provides a specific structure showing what to eat if you want to have high energy and vitality. Books like this one can trigger a Conversation for Structure that will produce successful results when implemented.

Structure is for function. We learned that in anatomy class. Our bones enable our bodies to have form. Without structure we could not move. This type of conversation provides the bones, the structure for our goals or desired outcomes to come alive.

I encouraged a client, Shelley, to create a Conversation for Structure with her whole team after her company sales territories were realigned. Her team was now responsible for double the number of states it had before, and she now had a new boss. These unexpected changes had thrown off Shelley's normal calm state of mind. I pointed out to Shelley that when there is a gap between where we are and where we need to be, it's a signal that a Conversation for Structure is needed. That's how we fill in the gap. This territory change created several days of confusion, and team members needed to know how to operate and what was now expected of them. Initially Shelley was thinking she would wait for her new boss to fill in how he wanted things aligned since she did not know him well. But hundreds of customers were without an assigned representative, which threatened to cause more problems if it did not get addressed quickly.

I pointed out to Shelley that since she is the manager for the region, she needed to figure out the "how" of the structure herself, while her new boss got his feet on the ground in his new role. After our discussion, she began the conversation by engaging her whole team. "We are now responsible for all sales activity in Florida, Georgia, Alabama, and Mississippi in addition to the states we had previously," she said, and then she offered some suggestions. "Sam, you take all the accounts that start with letters A–F; Jane, you take all the accounts G–L . . . Do you agree this would work? . . . How many existing customers would that immediately give each of you? Would each of your figure that out in the next 24 hours and get back to me with the numbers and your ideas for next steps?" By initiating this conversation, Shelley added structure and got the members of her team focused on what they needed to be doing.

Conversations Done Right

Here are some examples of how it sounds when a Conversation for Structure is done well.

Cynthia and Hema

Cynthia Kyriazis is a professional organizer and time management consultant who works on my team at The Professional Development Group. She has a structured approach to organizing paper, time, and space so that people meet their own goals. She is a masterful coach who can process individuals through their own thinking to create a structure for increased efficiency. Let's listen into a conversation where she coaches Hema, the director of public relations and community affairs.

Hema: *I am struggling with being overwhelmed in my work. I don't know what my priorities are because I have so much on my plate that seems urgent. I don't remember what I have promised I will do, because I write things down in several places and then can't remember where it is. Things keep slipping through the cracks, and I can tell the CEO is annoyed with me because I did not follow up with him last week. I know you are an expert in productivity, and I really need help changing this situation.*

Cynthia: *Let's start with an organizing principle that will provide structure for you so you can more easily manage the demands of all this paper I see in your office. Are you familiar with the saying, "Have a place for everything and keep everything in its place"?*

Hema: *Yes, I am, but you can tell by looking at my office that I am not sure how to do that.*

Cynthia: *Let's talk about how this organizing principle applies to you. Imagine you are in your kitchen. If I blindfolded you, would you know where the spoons are? How about the plates, the glasses, the pots and pans?*

Hema: *Yes, I am faithful about putting each of them back in their place when I unload the dishwasher.*

Cynthia: *Exactly. You have a system in your kitchen that groups similar things together. This system enables you to be creative and chaotic while cooking, but productive because you go back to your system at the end. By returning everything to its designated space, you can turn around and repeat that process the next day. The same thing can happen in your work environment. It means sorting papers so you create a defined space for retrieving those papers when you need them. Here is how it will work. The CEO stops by your office and suggests that you follow up on an article that was in the New York Times last week. He gives you the article, and it goes into this inbox. The thing I want you to remember is that sorting is the basis of all time management programs. Think about it; doesn't your calendar simply act as a sorting tool to help you sort your time? If you sort or block time daily to focus on priorities, planning, or even cleaning up your kitchen, it helps you improve your productivity because it gives you a structure and process for managing during a chaotic, busy day. Given the flow of your day, I suggest that you set aside one hour at the beginning of each day and three hours every Friday*

afternoon to prioritize and process what is in your inbox and to review
your projects list. Is this a structure you can live with?
Hema: *Yes, I think I can do this.*
Cynthia: *Let's focus on the steps of how you do this by looking at your*
schedule and how you currently have your time allocated . . . I'd like you
to keep a time log for the next week so we can look at the way you used
your time.

Curt

Curt, a project manager in a pharmaceutical company, was
responsible for working with the marketing teams to assure all
operational activities were taken care of to meet new marketing
goals. For one initiative, the marketing team knew it wanted to
extend the product line to include a 5-milligram tablet. The
company already had a 2.5-milligram tablet and realized patients
were taking two of these, and so it made sense to create a 5-mil-
ligram tablet. The company did not know how to make it happen because doubling the size of the tablet was not reasonable.
As a result, Curt's role was to create Conversations for Structure
with the various operational groups within the organization.
Over a series of several Conversations for Structure in five meetings, in which Curt proposed some of the steps and others commented and built on his ideas, Curt ensured that all the activities
that needed to be done were identified and carried out to create
the new 5-milligram tablet within the time frame established
by the marketing team. Curt's ability to craft individual and
group Conversations for Structure enabled the vision to come
alive for this pharmaceutical company.

Phrases and Questions to Start a Conversation

Here are some ways to get your Conversation for Structure
started:

- "Now that we are clear on the goal, how do we see this
  evolving?"

- "What things need to happen for success?"
- "Here is how we are going to move forward . . ."
- "What are the priorities? Of all the possibilities, what are the three most important steps that need to occur early on?"
- "What structure needs to be put in place up front?"
- "Which of these steps are absolutely necessary, and why?"
- "Who are the people that need to be involved?"
- "Is there a timeline for the steps? When does each step need to be completed by?"
- "Do we need to create a project charter or statement of work, and how will it be done? Would it be useful to put it into a visual map?"
- "How will we track our progress?"
- "What are the cost constraints that we need to be aware of, and how do they impact our structure?"
- "What are some of the best practices we could use for our structure?"
- "What does the timeline for deliverables look like? How often will we . . . ?"
- "I am sending out the agenda prior to the meeting so everyone knows what is expected when we are together."
- "Who will keep notes, serve as the time tracker, and facilitate key discussions?"
- Have we mapped each step to the calendar to ensure that we don't have something due on a holiday or when we are all at a conference?"
- "Is there a data dashboard we'd like to look at weekly or monthly to track our progress?"
- "Have we identified the project stakeholders and gotten their input on the steps that need to be taken?"
- "Is there a specific sequence that needs to be in place?"
- "What already exists that will make what we are trying to create easier? Do we need to make any changes to the existing processes to fit in with what we are doing?"

With someone who has read this book or attended the seminar: "I'd like to have a Conversation for Structure. When would be a good time for you to do that?"

Mistakes in Conversation

Starting a relationship with a Conversation for Structure is risky because it does not build a connection or establish a big picture about why we are choosing this possibility. A nurse may tell the patient how to do three specific things to prepare for the doctor's exam, or a technical support representative may tell the customer how to follow several steps to solve the problem the customer is calling about—each of these conversations is just what is needed at that time; however, it does not build a long-term connection. When we want a long-term relationship with the person, we need to begin with a Conversation for Connection and a Conversation for Creating New Possibilities. A Conversation for Structure needs to follow, rather than being the starting point for a long-term relationship. This is a mistake that new managers make too often. People who are overly focused on tactical implementation often want to start with a Conversation for Structure, while people who are overly focused on the big picture frequently skip over this conversation completely.

Consultants or independent project managers often struggle with this conversation early on in a new relationship with a client. They ask me, "If I explain step-by-step what I will be doing, what is preventing the clients from just doing that themselves and not using me?" This is a reasonable concern when it feels like the person or company you are considering working with is shopping you. It has happened to me as well. I've found early on in the process of engaging with a new client that it is useful to describe the outcomes we want to create and agree that we'll lay out all the steps to create the results after the contract or agreement has been signed. Sometimes this works, and other times the prospect requires each step of the work to be described in detail. When that happens, the consultant has to decide if he or she wants to put this conversation into place at that time or not.

Joyce, the director of sales for a small advertising company, shared with me that one of the challenges she faced in her work was that it was not easy for customers to buy her company's services. When we looked closely at the conversations she and her company were having with prospects, we realized the Conversation for Structure was missing. Prospects heard the big-picture possibility clearly but did not understand how it would be implemented in a logical way they could follow. They could not see the "package" of services that provided a structure. Joyce decided to create a visual map that showed the steps and the outcomes from each step. She began to use this map at the point in the conversation with prospects where they asked, "How will your company be able to do this?" She handed them the map and walked them through it step-by-step. Now she had the tools to show the specific steps clearly. Putting this conversation in place enabled Joyce to dramatically increase the number of prospects who became customers.

When There's No Conversation

The following problems can result when the Conversation for Structure is missing:

- We may have agreement on a goal or concept, but we may not be on the same page about how it will be done.
- There is no clarity about the process, steps, timetable, or sequence of events.
- We do not know how to do what we want done.
- Frustration bubbles up because it is not clear how to implement the actions needed to move forward.

Sometimes we do not have all the steps clearly defined. For example, we know we are going to hold a conference at the convention center, but there are a dozen conference halls there and a dozen ways we could get there. We might propose various options for where we could hold the meeting and how we could get there. Depending on where we are or what is expected of us, we may leave it at that until other decisions are made and it is clear we need to identify the next step in the structure.

Final Words

When we know what we want to create, the next step is to create a plan for how to get there. Creating forward movement or momentum is the intention. Be open and wise enough to bring in additional people to help you move through what does not come naturally to you. A colleague, manager, peer, or coach can help you when you are stuck. It is not uncommon for people to set big goals without thinking through how they will bring the goals alive. In fact, this happens regularly in the Conversation for Creating New Possibilities. We need to follow that conversation with a focus on structure for momentum to occur.

Although some people, at the start of a new relationship, begin the communication with a Conversation for Structure, when we want a long-term relationship, a Conversation for Connection and a Conversation for Creating New Possibilities also need to be initiated.

Conversation for Commitment

When we have a plan or structure in place, and we've identified the action steps, we can ask, "Who will do each step?" We identify who will be responsible for each step, and then we ask each person if he or she is willing to perform it. On other occasions we realize we want to change something that will require us to commit to new actions. Perhaps the organization in which you work has made a new commitment to going green. Team leaders ask employees in departmental meetings if they will begin to use the recycle containers and stop ordering plastic bags. "Will you commit to doing your part in our green effort by using a mug instead of a plastic cup?" the manager asks each team member individually. Without this specific conversation, it is often not clear exactly what actions are expected.

Use this conversation when:

- Asking someone to play a role on your team or board, or following up from a meeting in which next actions were identified
- Asking a boss or senior manager to support a proposal or idea you want to move forward with

- Gaining alignment among team members toward a common goal
- Being clear on what you stand for
- Knowing who is responsible for what
- Being clear on what it means to keep your word
- Demonstrating integrity (walking your talk)

All about Commitment

Disengagement is the opposite of commitment. When people feel fear or anger, it can trigger them to disengage instead of commit or take a clear stand. A recent Gallup study estimates that employee disengagement results in over $300 billion in lost productivity in the United States. This study also says that more than 50 percent of current employees are disengaged in their work. When employees do not feel valued, they will not commit themselves to their work or the organization.

The Disney organization gets executives engaged immediately when they are hired by having them dress in a character costume and march in an afternoon parade. The new managers experience firsthand how excited families are to be part of the Disney magic. The new managers also begin to see how their decisions impact the people who keep the magic alive at Disney.

One way I've seen clients keep employees engaged is to share with them in town hall meetings what the current reality is and ask for suggestions and ideas. Asking, "What do you think we need to commit to as an organization? What are you willing to commit to as a result of our current reality?" engages all levels of the organization. I watched an organization do this when its health-care costs rose sharply. The employees were shown the financial realities and asked to suggest ways to deal with this so the organization could continue to grow and be profitable. Employees asked for a la carte health-care services and agreed to increase the amount they paid out of pocket. Because they came up with the recommendation, they were committed to the outcomes.

To keep employees committed, make sure their priorities are clear and their workload is doable. If employees feel they are trusted and respected, they will more likely stay committed to dialogue about what their current reality is and what they are focused on creating. Some of the things that cause people to disengage include:

- Working for leaders who do not experience the consequences of their decisions
- Experiencing a loss of trust in relationships with managers and peers
- Feeling spied on or micromanaged
- Having unclear priorities with unrealistic deadlines

Taking a Stand

When we take a stand and make it clear with our words and actions, it is easier to get other people inspired to make a change too. Many companies have made a commitment to using natural, earth-friendly products. Others have committed to reducing printing to save paper, trees, and money. One manager I worked with told his team he had decided to stop printing e-mails, and instead he would carry his laptop into meetings in case he needed to reference something. After doing this for some time, he then asked his peers individually if they would stop printing e-mails unless it was absolutely necessary. His words and actions created an ongoing Conversation for Commitment in his organization.

Method is a company that creates earth-friendly cleaning products. The owners of this company have made a clear stand to use natural ingredients and to be green in everything they do. When they made this stand, they communicated it publicly, inviting their customers to follow along. They regularly conduct Conversations for Commitment with their employees and customers.

If we have not thought out our stand for how we want to communicate in our professional lives, we are probably on autopilot, reacting based on what happens. Successful people have commitments they make to themselves and to others. The commitments we make to ourselves about who we want to be are the most fundamental commitments we will make.

Mark, a wealth manager in a large brokerage firm, was told by one of his clients that he lacked the listening skills needed to make his clients think of him as a trusted advisor. Mark called me and asked me if I would help him develop strong listening skills. Before I began working with Mark, I created a Conversation for Commitment with him. It went something like this:

Shawn: *Mark, I hear you saying you want to develop stronger listening skills so that you will be seen as a trusted advisor by your clients and prospects, right?*

Mark: *Yes, I've been told by more than one person that I interrupt too often and that I talk too much. I know I need to learn how to ask better questions and really tune into what the prospect or client is saying.*

Shawn: *What are the outcomes you want to create by changing your current communication patterns?*

Mark: *I'd like my clients to feel like I really heard what was important to them. I'd like to ensure that my own comments are directed at what clients really need rather than me rambling on and on. I want to earn that "trusted advisor" title with all my clients and prospects.*

Shawn: *I'll provide you with specific actions to take in conversations with clients and prospects, and you can take notes in a communication journal. Will you practice the activities each day and record your observations in the journal I will give you? In order to make this change, Mark, are you willing to commit to working on your communication skills daily for the next 90 days?*

Mark: *Yes, I will agree to that commitment.*

One of my favorite inspiring quotes speaks to the importance of being clear on your commitments. W. H. Murray wrote the following during one of the first Himalayan expeditions:

> Until one is committed, there is hesitancy, the chance to draw back, always ineffectiveness. Concerning all acts of initiative (and creation), there is one elementary truth, the ignorance of which kills countless

ideas and splendid plans: that the moment one definitely commits oneself, then providence moves too. A whole stream of events issues from the decision, raising in one's favor all manner of unforeseen incidents, meetings, and materials assistance, which no man could have dreamt would have come his way.

What are you committed to? Have you written it out in language that is inspiring to you? Do you read your goals or intention statement to yourself daily? Every morning before I begin my workday, I read my goals and my commitments to myself about who I want to be for myself and others. For example, my first commitment is to serve people in ways that are meaningful to both of us, and so on my daily list my first line is "What can I do today to serve someone meaningfully?" This is a good reminder to myself about what I am committed to doing. Answering this question inspires me and triggers the feeling of hope for me.

Forgetting What You Are Committed To

Sometimes we forget our commitments to ourselves, and we lose our awareness of being in the present moment. Yesterday my coaching client Judy shared this with me:

> I caught myself in a new awareness. I work with a project manager who is assigned to my client team. We have a "toxic relationship." What I mean by that is we habitually trigger the worst in each other and really do not know each other today as a result. I label the relationship based on past experience, and by doing this I keep the relationship stuck in that pattern. I realize this about the interaction on one level, and I forget it and get suckered into reacting sometimes. This "toxic relationship" label was attached to this person before I created a stand about what I want in my relationships with my colleagues. Now it is time for me to clean up this mixed message I am sending myself and clean up the relationship with the project manager.
>
> In the presence of toxic peers, overbearing bosses, and employees who forget the years of good manners they've known, sometimes I

forget what I am committed to in my own professionalism. I lose my stand. Out of fear I go back into a click-whirl form of autopilot that precedes my decision to create a better way of living and emotional intelligence.

Judy is making great progress in her own self-awareness and her ability to self-regulate. Her stand is becoming clearer to herself.

What does it look like when people seemingly forget who they are? They act inconsistently. Everything you know about them disappears. I sometimes call this "coming out sideways." In other words, any time people are not being aware, direct, and clear in their actions, words, and behavior—when they are out of integrity with who they say they are—this is *coming out sideways*. People can get into the past so deeply they can't even remember there is a now. To get yourself back into integrity, write down your commitments and read them every day. Conversations for Commitment hold you and others accountable for what you want to accomplish, in solution-focused, positive language.

Sometimes it is easier to see when someone else forgets who he or she is than it is to recognize when you are doing so. There is a dramatic discrepancy between who the person is most of the time and how the person behaves in a specific situation. Here is an example:

A manager was talking with an employee who had told a little white lie and done something he should not have done. If she had asked him a few questions, such as "How are you feeling about this?" "How could you clean this situation up now?" "What would you do differently if faced with a similar situation again?" he would have come up with his own answers to repair his damage.

Instead, she forgot the importance of emotional awareness and preferred communication styles. She began berating him, "You are a liar, and I will not trust you again after this." She temporarily forgot that ordinarily he was a very good employee and also that he was very young and testing his boundaries. This was the first time she had seen this behavior from him. She labeled him as a liar and told him he was not worthy of trust. She forgot who he really was, and she saw the worst in him. If she could remember that he is a young person who is trying to find his way with his commitment about who he is professionally and that he needs guidance, not labels, she will help him far more. She could be the inspiring manager who is committed to development. She needs to remember her commitment or her stand. She needs to engage in a conversation that says, "I've known you for two years. I know this recent experience is not who you are. A little white lie breaks trust, and you are usually someone who builds trust. What do you want to do about this situation? How do you think we can rebuild the trust?" This shift in conversation will change the way he experiences his job and what happens in their relationship.

A manager who loses sight of the vision for the team, an employee who keeps searching for a new position after she's accepted a new position and has only been in the job for a month, a father who works nonstop and has not seen his child play baseball—these are examples of people who forgot what they were committed to or what they stand for. Taking a stand means drawing a line in the sand and revealing what side you are on.

Staying Committed Means Making Tough Decisions

Gene is committed to being a manager who is focused on the development and support of his employees. He and his team designed a six-week new-hire training program that had a comprehensive exam at the end of it. He was clear in the recruiting efforts that new hires would have to pass the training and the exam to continue employment. He knew the test worked; if people passed it, they were contributing members of the team. If they couldn't pass the test, they weren't going to add value to the team and would take up too much of the managers' time to be worth keeping on the team. One young man, Bill, had the initial skills and abilities they were looking for in a team member. Yet when Bill was in the class, he did not apply himself. He

109

did not participate in the discussions and was not engaging himself fully. Therefore, it did not come as a surprise to Gene when Bill failed the test.

Gene delivered the news this way: "Bill, this test score is not a reflection of who you are as a person. It is a snapshot in time that says you did not apply yourself enough to be able to keep this position. It is not a sentence about your future. You can choose to do something entirely different that triggers passion and enthusiasm in you so that you are excited about what you do every day. What you now know is that this job is not it." Bill said, "Are you firing me?" Gene said, "Yes."

A few days later, Gene got a note from Faith, the manager who was seated in the meeting when he had this conversation to fire Bill. Faith said that it was the most compassionate firing she'd ever seen and that Gene gave Bill a way to save face and create something better for his future. Faith said if she ever had to fire an employee, she would remember this experience. A month later, Gene got a note from Bill thanking him for the way he showed Bill that this was not the best path for him. Most of the people Gene has fired have written him thank you notes later, saying that the conversation made a huge difference in the way they moved forward next. The story he frames about why they are being fired emphasizes the idea that this specific experience did not work, not that they are being fired because of who they are as people. This is a stand for compassion even in the face of delivering bad or unwanted news.

When we label an employee as a bad performer, it may be that we are not asking for what we want and taking a stand for the employee's development. There are times when we have to dramatically draw a line in the sand to get someone's attention. When our stand is clear, we are better able to do that. Momentum comes from being clear in your stand and living it in the moment.

When we are blaming someone else for what is happening to us, we are not taking a stand for ourselves. I once watched an interaction between two professionals that played out like this:

she bashed him when he was not in the room; she resented his behavior; she criticized and belittled him constantly. It made others uncomfortable to be in their presence because of the way she behaved aggressively toward him and the way he did nothing to change the dynamics that occurred between them. This interaction went on like this for years. Neither took a stand for what they wanted for themselves. Instead, they held to their stand that the other person was wrong. He was too passive, and she was too aggressive. They were intent on their stand blaming the other person, and they didn't enjoy or appreciate each other despite working together for years. Their relationship did not have to be this destructive, but neither knew how to change the conversation pattern to create something better because they did not have a commitment to do so.

Do you have a commitment to yourself about who you want to be as a professional? What is your stand on how you converse with your employees, boss, colleagues? Are you interacting based on past labels, or are you being present in the moment to who the other person is now and who you are now? Managers, coaches, fund-raisers, board members, and project managers must engage in Conversations for Commitment in order to do the core of their job.

Conversations Done Right

Here are some examples of how it sounds when a Conversation for Commitment goes well.

Mark and Alison

Mark Jones is a manager working in an organization that has a strong commitment to developing future leaders. One of Mark's team members, Alison, had not made it clear to Mark what her career goals were. At the time he saw great potential in her. But he could not determine if she saw this in herself or was interested in being part of the high-potential fast-track group. To distinguish what she wanted for her own career and her professional development plan, Mark asked, "Alison, what do you want to create for your own career path? What are you committed to in terms of your own professional development?"

His questions began a dialogue to get her to explore her own vision for herself. Mark told Alison that he saw great potential in her and would be willing to commit to support her if she were offered a slot in the company's high-potential group. This Conversation for Commitment impacted Alison's expectations and vision of herself—she raised the bar of her own expectations. As a result, she began to demonstrate more confidence and volunteer for more challenging assignments. Within three months of the initial conversation, Alison was invited into the company's high-potential development track.

Carly

Sometimes we can see a possible commitment or stand that would make a difference for someone else. Imagine the flow of this situation: a colleague, Carly, is struggling with her new boss. Carly is judging her new boss's communication and management style based on her former boss's style. The new boss has a completely different management style than her prior manager and is requiring many adjustments in the way information is shared. Currently Carly is focusing on the negative and playing the complaint game. She seems unaware that her stand appears to be making her new boss wrong or bad.

As you are in conversation with Carly, you see two beliefs that would help her. You share your own stand with her that (1) change is normal and will be an ongoing part of business and (2) when we have a new boss, we also have a new job. When we accept this reality, it enables us to create a more useful stand in finding ways to support the new boss and the current reality. So, next you ask her, "Carly, are you committed to finding a way to make this work with your new boss?" Then you engage her in a dialogue about what her stand really is. This is an example of processing someone through her commitments. Watch and listen closely to the answer. Sometimes words and body language do not match. When that happens, it is useful to ask more questions.

Sara

As a department manager, Sara has found it is very useful to regularly evaluate her commitments by checking in with others about their perceptions. Sara realizes that if she is not walking her talk, it means she is not taking a stand for her commitments. Sara appreciates having a strong and open communication channel with people. She asks, "How are we doing in our relationship? . . . What would you like more of or less of . . . from me? What could I do to be more supportive of you?" She asks these questions to her employees, peers, customers, and senior management.

Sara listens when they give her feedback. She never explains or tries to justify why she has done or has failed to do something. No matter what the other person says, she replies, "Thank you for sharing your feedback with me." She takes a few days and lets it settle in. She looks for themes and trends so as to keep her own self-awareness high.

Sometimes she will write a thank you note because someone was courageous enough to point out to her that she was coming out sideways or off her stand. When getting a message like this, a few days later she circles back and says something like "I've decided to take action on . . ." to share what she will do with the feedback she received. This causes others to see that she is also taking a stand for her own growth as well as the ongoing relationship with them.

Sara regularly has people compliment her management style. I've heard people tell her that she is the best manager they've ever worked for because of the clear commitment she has to the relationship. Her stand is clear.

Phrases and Questions to Start a Conversation

Here are some ways to get your Conversation for Commitment started:

- "Would you be interested in these outcomes?"
- "Are you willing to . . . ?"
- "Can I count on you to do . . . ?"
- "The reason this is so important to us is . . . As a result, would you agree to . . . ?"
- "I need your help on the XYZ project; can I count on you to do . . . ?"
- "Will you be able to show Peshi around the department on her first day next Tuesday? Will you let me know how it went when you are finished?"
- "One of the commitments we made several months ago was . . . , and we are still committed to these outcomes."
- "We are looking for a commitment of 20 hours dedicated to this project in the next week. Are you able to do this?"
- "The proposal calls for $5,000 for the next phase in the work we want to do. Will you agree to have that come from your department budget?"
- "Andy, the board has decided it would like you to lead the marketing effort. Here is an outline of the specific accountabilities expected of this role."
- "When we launch a new initiative but fail to follow through, we create a cultural norm that commitment is not important. What can we do now to demonstrate we are committed to this initiative over the next six months? How can we prompt ourselves to talk about it 6, 9, and 12 months from now to demonstrate this is not another flavor-of-the-day effort?"

Mistakes in Conversation

A common mistake is not asking people if they are committed because you assume they have the same passion for the project that you do. Leaders should not delegate the responsibility for ensuring commitment from the team to others. Look your employees in the eye and ask, "Have you agreed to do this? Are you committed to completing the XYZ project?"

If we do not show how actions taken today are based on seeds planted by past initiatives, we do not reinforce the importance of our commitments. I watched an organization make a significant commitment to teaching its workforce goal-setting and measurement techniques to track progress against the organization's strategic initiatives. Every manager went through training, and then the managers led workshops for their own teams, embedding the goal-setting and measurement-tracking processes into their work. This was both expensive and time consuming for this large organization, but it paid off with results in alignment in goals and increased profit. Nine months later I randomly heard comments from employees, saying things like "That goal-setting and measurement stuff we did was just another flavor-of-the-day thing management made us do." When I heard that, I was stunned, because the organization was still using the process and techniques. In the very department where these words were being spoken, there were measurement boards with the goals listed at the top and the current data hanging on the wall for everyone in the department to see. In addition, the results were also posted on the company's intranet. Connect the dots for people verbally and in writing so they see that actions that are being taken today are based on commitments that were made months and years ago.

When There's No Conversation

The following problems can result when the Conversation for Commitment is missing:

- We do not feel committed.
- We do not feel like we have ownership.
- We do not know who is responsible for what.
- It is not clear to team members who is making the decisions or how the decision process will work.

Final Words

When we have a plan with the identified action steps, we can then identify who are the right people to do what needs to be done. We need to ask clearly for what we want and then ask if they are willing to commit to take the actions needed to produce the desired outcomes.

If we have not thought out our own stand and what we are committed to, then we are likely working from someone else's agenda or are reacting like a firefighter to whatever shows up in front of us. Successful people have commitments they make to themselves and to others. The commitments we make to ourselves about who we want to be are the most fundamental commitments we will make.

When you are being clear in your stand and living in the moment based on what you are committed to, you'll find momentum and the joy of growth, and others will respect you for it.

CHAPTER 9

Conversation for Action

Once you have explored your options and know what you want to create and how to do it, we flow into this conversation about action. What do you want to *do*? What do you need to do to bring your dreams and goals alive? After you have done that, then what will you do next? Asking these questions is a way of processing ourselves or others through our own thinking.

Use this conversation when:

- You have agreed to a goal and are ready to move forward.
- You are ready to get things done.
- You see the next step that needs to be completed.
- You need to identify the next actions that need to be done to move forward.

All about Action

Earlier I challenged you to come up with a list of 100 things and experiences you wanted to create. Making this list is a profound experience in having your own stand. You begin to see patterns and realize what you want that was not clear before writing out the list. Knowing what experiences and outcomes you want to create leads to a confidence that is palpable. Perhaps some of the items you'll add to the list will be the conversations you want to create with specific people in your life and new people you want to meet.

The items on this list are possibilities that could become your projects or goals. One of my favorite questions when working on a project was one I learned from David Allen, author of *Getting Things Done: The Art of Stress-Free Productivity.* The magic question is "What is the next action needed?" This question is so powerful because it enables us to clearly see the next step and then move into action. In the midst of any project, this is a conversation worth having with your team members once each week. Similarly, you'll want to have Conversations for Action while working through your list of all the things and experiences you want to create.

I've watched people get stuck in a project because they do not know what to do next. When this happens, they are not asking themselves the right questions. It only takes seconds to ask this question and generate new thinking. The next action needed may be something like:

- Go talk with others who have accomplished what you want to do. Ask them how they did it and what they did when they were at the stage where you are now.
- Search online for others who are currently doing what you want to do. How are they creating success?
- Recall a time when you were stuck before. What did you do to move forward? Could you do that now?

If you don't know what the next step is, then figuring out the next step *is* your next step. Having a Conversation for Action will help you find clarity when you are unsure what needs to be done next. When you have moments of clarity about what you want to accomplish, write it down. The act of writing helps crystallize your thinking and hone that clarity further.

Sometimes you might wake up in the middle of the night with an idea. It's good to keep a paper and pen next to the bed so you can capture the idea that you want to take action on.

Other times, you might be in a meeting and an idea flashes in your mind about something you want to do. That's why it is a good idea to keep a notebook that is specifically used for tracking your "To Do" or "Next Action" list.

Managers, coaches, and counselors of all kinds regularly engage in Conversations for Action. Conversations are exchanges with ourselves or others in which we process thinking. In this process we move our thinking to the next level so that it is actionable. That is what enables us to be productive, because we are clear on the action to take to bring our goals alive.

Conversations Done Right

Here are some examples of how it sounds when a Conversation for Action goes well.

Rita

Rita Charlestein is an entrepreneurial go-getter who has owned and led several businesses. She keeps herself and her clients organized and focused. She has daily conversations with her staff about what the top three priorities are for the business and what actions everyone needs to take to make them happen. It is clear in a conversation with her that she is confident, focused, and productive because of her clarity about what she is doing now and why. Let's drop in on an early morning meeting with one of her team members, Juan.

Rita: *Hi Juan, I've been thinking about the Campbell's project; we need to get marketing data sent to them by Friday. What can we do to ensure that we're on time with this?*

Juan: *I need to download the current data, review it for inconsistencies, and then put it into a file format that can be sent to them.*

Rita: *OK, sounds good. After that's done, what will be the next step?*

Juan: *I need to ask them who they want it sent to so I have all the e-mail addresses and know which format would be best for them.*

Rita: *Good. Juan, how long are you estimating it will take for you to perform those steps? … If there is anything else you need from me today to move this forward, just let me know, OK?*

Rita then moves on to a conversation with her head of sales, Zachary:

Rita: *Zachary, how are things coming with the proposal to IMS?*

Zachary: *We have the first two parts completed.*

Rita: *What is the next action needed?*

Zachary: *I need to get the numbers from Mark and the shipping information from Michelle to put into the proposal.*

Rita: *Good. Is that a priority for you today, or has something else bubbled up?*

Zachary: *Glad you asked. I meant to tell you that Jim from Merck called at the end of the day yesterday and asked us for a proposal for another three months' extension on what we are already doing for them. They need it as soon as possible because they are going into a meeting this afternoon and will need the costs associated with extending the work. I am going to focus on that first and then go back to the proposal for IMS.*

Rita: *Good thinking, Zachary. Let me know if I can help with anything.*

Reviewing the current projects list and asking what the next action needed for each project is may sound very simple, but it is also very powerful. *What are the options in what we could do today? What is the next action? Then what?* If you ask these three questions of your staff and let them process their own thinking as a result of the questions, you will see ways to progress. Try it now by asking yourself these questions.

Karen

Karen was a new manager for a team that had the lowest productivity numbers of all the teams in her midsized company. She had been moved over to manage this team because she had a track record of success. She knew how to get teams focused on action. Her manager said he did not know why this team couldn't get its act together since individually each person on the team had the know-how to do his or her job. After two days observing the group, Karen noticed the team members did not meet together after lunch. She asked one of the team members, "Why doesn't the group continue to work together after the lunch break?" The reply she got was, "It's simple. Brian stinks after lunch." Brian loved to play tennis, and he would squeeze in a match whenever he could. He kept his tennis gear in the back of his car so at lunch he could meet someone on the court for 40 minutes before returning to work. As a result, Brian stunk. Yes, that is right—he smelled of body odor. In the afternoons his teammates could smell him from a few feet away. Apparently, they hadn't mentioned this to him, but they complained and made fun of him behind his back.

When Karen realized that Brian's body odor was impacting this team's productivity, rather than shutting down and being afraid to address the real issue as prior managers had been, she had a Conversation for Action. She understood the next action she needed to take to change this situation, and it involved a difficult conversation. On the way home from work that evening, she bought a new bottle of antiperspirant and deodorant.

The next morning she asked Brian to talk privately. She looked him in the eye and asked him if there was any medical reason why he would not be able to use the product, which was on her desk. "Of course not," he said. "I do use it in the mornings after I shower, but perhaps I need to use it again after I play tennis at lunch when I do not have access to a shower?" She put the deodorant into a bag and asked him to take it with him and to begin using it after he exercised during breaks from work. Although he seemed a little embarrassed, he agreed to start doing so. That was the last time they talked about it, and there has not been an issue since. She then invited the members of the team to meet that afternoon. There was no foul smell to distract their focus. The next afternoon, she pulled the team together again and had the members focus on another part of their work together. With her direction, they were now being more productive, meeting often throughout the whole day.

Sometimes it takes courage to implement the next action we see that needs to be taken. Wise managers and leaders do not shy away from the next Conversation for Action they need to have, even if it may be uncomfortable or challenging.

Phrases and Questions to Start a Conversation

Here are some ways to get your Conversation for Action started:

- "What is the next action needed to move this forward?"
- "What will you do next?"
- "Then what? Then what?"
- "What is the priority now?"
- "What is the next step?"
- "Imagine that failure is taken out of the picture. In other words, if you will not fail, what would you do next?"
- "I've heard when you want to break a huge overwhelming goal down, it is useful to remember you eat an elephant only one bite at a time. What is one step we could take that would move us forward?"
- "Is there a map we could draw that would show us the sequence of action steps we want to take?"
- "Let's create a checklist so we can all see the action steps in front of us and check them off individually as they are completed."
- *With someone who has read this book or attended the When the Conversation Changes workshop:* "I'd like to have a Conversation for Action. When would be a good time for you to do that?"

Mistakes in Conversation

Demanding or forcing an answer does not work. If Juan told Rita he was stumped about what to do next, she would not say, "Well, just do something now." Instead she would move to a Conversation for Creating New Possibilities and play out various options that could occur.

Giving employees specific direction about what action needs to be done next is a wise idea when they are new in the job. However, there is a time when the employees begin to think for themselves about what actions need to be done. If a manager keeps specifying the next action to be taken, the manager will be micromanaging—not guiding. As a manager, if you find yourself in this situation, ask the questions given in the previous section instead of telling the employees what the next step is. This will lead to a new level of thinking and proactive behavior.

Processing people through their own thinking is a skill. It is the skill that distinguishes an outstanding manager or coach from a mediocre one. When we do not use questions to process employees or team members through their thinking, we are missing an opportunity as a communicator. Becoming a trusted advisor to our bosses, clients, and colleagues requires this ability to ask questions that distill the priorities and next actions needed to bring them alive. When we do not know how to do this, we do not become trusted advisors.

When There's No Conversation

The following problems can result when the Conversation for Action is missing:

* Lacking clarity about what is important to do next
* Experiencing fuzzy thinking and a numbness to the tasks and projects that have been committed to
* Feeling overwhelmed by all that needs to be done and constantly feeling stressed
* Not being on the same page with peers, colleagues, managers, or team members about what is being done

When individuals, by themselves or as members of a team, do not engage in a Conversation for Action, they miss out on momentum, and they do not make decisions that propel them forward. The lack of clarity causes a reactive state of mind and work habits. People who are operating this way do not likely have the tools to focus both strategically and tactically without missing important details.

Final Words

Once you have explored your options and know how you're going to proceed, you naturally flow into a Conversation for Action. "What is the next action needed?" is a magic question that enables us to keep the momentum going. If we are not sure of the answer to this question, then we must ask, "Who would know what the next action needs to be? How can I ask that person? Or could we move to a Conversation for Creating New Possibilities to explore options?"

When you have moments of clarity about what you want to accomplish, write them down. Keep an ongoing list of what you want to do and create for all the areas of your life. The act of writing these goals down will help crystallize your thinking and hone your clarity.

CHAPTER 10

Conversation for Accountability

After a Conversation for Commitment has occurred and the expectations are clear, being accountable for what you want to do is a sign of personal respect. If other people are involved, such as when you are part of a team, being accountable is also a sign of respect toward others. Accountability brings authority and responsibility into alignment.

Use this conversation when:

- Coaching an employee, peer, or colleague to stay focused on the previously defined goals
- Debriefing a team on what has been accomplished
- Reviewing your own goals and commitments
- Spinning around in a goal that has not yet moved forward
- Holding yourself accountable for what you agreed to do
- Holding others accountable for what they agreed to do
- Talking about the impact when others do not live up to their promises

All about Accountability

What are the most important actions you need to take in order to complete your goals? Even more important than the individual steps is the matter of being held accountable for the results. A lot can go wrong on the path of putting together a project, and sometimes personal responsibility can become a giant roadblock. Let's take a look at the story of one of my clients. Keiko, a leader in a pharmaceutical company, was stumped by Tim, one of her best task-oriented performers. Keiko realized that she was responsible for her whole team, and therefore she needed to be accountable for the outcomes created by her direct report Tim.

Tim was a workhorse who would regularly put in 10- to 12-hour days analyzing reports and data. He was very task focused and never missed a deadline with his research work. The issue Keiko was struggling with was Tim's sarcasm, his jabbing humor that had a put-down in it for others. He was often a difficult person to deal with interpersonally. He would lash out in anger and attack others with data. He was not aware of the emotional wake he left behind, and he showed no empathy for others. His colleagues often felt judged and put down within a few minutes of interacting with him.

As Tim's manager, Keiko needed him to be able to interact with people without interpersonal issues cropping up each time he was on a team project. Keiko tried to point out to Tim that how you make people feel is often more important to them than the specific content of the message. When she did this, he reacted defensively and went on the attack, pointing out things that others were doing wrong. Keiko realized that as Tim's manager, she needed to hold him accountable for improving his interpersonal communication even though he was not owning up to the issue. That is when Keiko called me. She asked me how she could get Tim to see his part in the interpersonal challenges he helped create instead of blaming others.

To drive accountability, you need to set clear objectives, measures, and boundaries, so that everyone is clear on what the expectations, consequences, and rewards are associated with the responsibilities. To encourage accountability, focus people on what they have done well. This energizes them, gets them focused on their own insights and wisdom, and gives them confidence that they can handle the change.
—Kathy Oates, VP Leadership and Organization Development at GlaxoSmithKline

I explained to Keiko that if Tim agreed to work with me as a coach, together we would raise his awareness about his interpersonal communication habits. Keiko explained to Tim that working with a coach on this issue was vital for his success. Tim agreed to the coaching but indicated that he was not aware of what he was doing that was causing the problem.

Awareness is the first step in holding people accountable. Tim did not understand the impact of his behavior, nor did he have a clear picture of what he needed to do differently. So I began working with Tim by showing him a video of interactions between people, and I asked him to point out which behaviors worked and which ones caused problems interpersonally. Because I knew Tim liked collecting data and doing research, I asked him to make a list of what he wanted to do and what he wanted to stop doing and to track this in his own behavior over a two-week period between our meetings.

Tim reported his observations as data points in our conversations. He had a clear picture of what to do and what not to do, and he began to count the number of times he phrased things in a way that acknowledged someone else's contribution instead of sarcastically putting the person down. Over several months Tim became aware of the emotional wake he left behind him and how others felt after meeting with him. He changed his interpersonal communication habits because we set up an accountability process for him through our biweekly meetings. A year later, Tim received an outstanding rating on his performance review because he had transformed his relationships with his peers.

> *People will forget what you said, people will forget what you did, but people will never forget how you made them feel.*
> —Maya Angelou

Accountability Partners

Sometimes when I set a long-term goal, it works better if I have an accountability partner. I've found it's easier to keep a commitment to a colleague than to myself. Once it is a habit, then I will keep the action going. I often serve as an accountability partner to my coaching clients, focusing on what they want to create in their interpersonal communication as a leader and manager.

Playing an accountability game that focuses on a project with someone who has an interest in accomplishing the same thing you do makes the process of achieving the goal even more fun. It triggers feelings of hope because there is support to reach the goal. Sarano Kelley wrote *The Game*, a book about how partners can hold each other accountable for a goal they want to achieve in 90 days. The book suggests that you find an accountability partner for a 90-day period, based on some theme or project you both want to focus on. You can support each other to create what you really want. This is the ultimate in building a foundation for momentum.

Here are some of the rules for accountability games you can play with professional colleagues:

- Focus for 30, 60, or 90 days. Agree to the time frame before starting.
- Don't criticize yourself or anyone else.
- Don't whine.
- Engage in meaningful activities with meaningful people.
- At the end of the day, reframe anything you've viewed as a failure, and accept that it is a step toward your success.

- Reward yourself and your partner throughout the game when you accomplish milestones.
- Break the big goals into smaller tasks, and give yourself rewards for each of the smaller tasks.
- Check in daily with your partner, read your commitment, and discuss what is working and what you will do next.
- Keep your game confidential.

The partner you select to play a game like this often determines the success of the game. Choose someone who wants to accomplish the same thing you do and who has a successful track record of accomplishment. If you cannot find someone like that, consider hiring a coach who already has expertise in the area in which you want to be held accountable.

A friend invited me to play *an accountability game* with her, and we created an amazing 90-day experience that led to great things for both of us. This experience inspired me to play an accountability game with my boss, colleagues, and team of employees who reported to me at the time. These 90-day games keep momentum flowing, enabling me to bring energy into all areas of my life, especially my work. One of the great things about playing an accountability game is that it provides a structure to stay connected. You know you're going to have a 10-minute conversation each day with your accountability partner, and you'll debrief each other on your progress. Staying connected during the game and holding each other accountable is simple because the structure is already in place.

Making Corrections

Occasionally, you may fall off your plan. If you have the resilience to get back on track, you can still steer yourself toward your goal. The key is having a Conversation for Accountability with a colleague you trust in order to discuss what has gone wrong and how you can fix the situation. High-performing professionals and companies willingly and effectively discuss when they or their team members are not on track with their goals. In poor-performing companies, ineffective employees are often ignored or transferred to another department without being held accountable for the mutually agreed-upon goals they committed to. Meaningful, open conversations at all levels within the organization lead to accountability.

Sometimes people we are responsible for need to be corrected or guided into creating a better outcome so that they are accountable for their own goals. If you manage other people, remember that respectful guidance and discipline for an employee who is not being accountable is important. One of the ways I do this is *to specifically ask for what I want.* For example: "Mark, I would like the presentation to be printed in full color, not black and white, please." Rather than clearly ask for what they want, too many people jump to complaining. The problem is that a complaint is nowhere near as effective as a clear request.

What happens, though, when the person doesn't do what was asked? In the example above, let's say Mark did not produce a full-color report. Circle back to Mark and say, "Help me to understand what happened. I was looking for this report in full color but got black and white." Then LISTEN. He may have an explanation, but I need to be willing to hear him. Maybe the color printer was broken or out of toner and he gave me the black and white so I at least had something during the meeting. When you don't get what you want from a work colleague, check in about what happened by repeating the desired request and stating, "Help me to understand what happened."

I know of an executive who actually wanted to fire a new employee who brought in a black-and-white report when he had been asked to make a color copy. The executive took it as an early warning that the new hire was lazy and unreliable. The new employee did not want to interrupt the meeting already in progress with a complaint about the copier, and so he did what he thought was best by delivering copies. Because the executive did not ask the question, he did not know the color copier was broken and the new employee was doing the best he could with the tools he had at the moment.

In my company, we have a mantra that reminds us to communicate when something changes: "How will you know if I do not tell you, and how will I know if you do not tell me?" Communication is the key to accountability. Keeping each other in the loop is vital for strong team spirit.

A Six-Step Plan for Confronting Others

Are you speaking up in a solution-focused manner when you notice something that could be improved? Does your organization encourage you to have Conversations for Accountability? Have you distinguished what causes some Conversations for Accountability to be more productive than others? Elizabeth Jeffries, an executive coach who focuses on executive mastery and works with me at The Professional Development Group, shares a six-step plan she uses to prepare for a Conversation for Accountability.

The plan is a multipurpose approach to dealing with other people's negative, ineffective, or unacceptable behavior. Sometimes you have to have a confrontation in order to obtain new outcomes in behavior.

1. *Approach* the person with an attitude of solving a problem rather than to put the person down. Do it at a time when you are in control of your emotions. This is the mental preparation step.
2. *Describe* the person's behavior objectively.
   "I have noticed/observed . . ."
3. *Express* your feelings and thoughts about the person's behavior.
   "I feel angry and frustrated."
4. *Suggest* a specific change in behavior.
   "I'd prefer/like . . ."
   "May I suggest . . ."
5. *Explain* the benefits that will result from the new behavior.
   "I'll be more open to your ideas . . ."

"If you will do that, we'll both be more effective in our work."

6. *Ask* for commitment to the new behavior.
"What would it take for you to . . . ?"
"Will you agree to this?"
"Can I count on you?"
If yes, ask, "How would I know?" *(the accountability statement)*

Practice Page for Confronting Others
For the practice page that follows, consider a situation with a team member that needs attention. Define the problem, and create a script to solve it using the confrontation ideas above. Practice.

The Importance of Confronting Others

Showing that we care makes a difference in how others hear us. Arbitrary discipline that is unclear, loud, mean, or judging will break trust and destroy relationships. It may trigger spiteful retaliation instead of the intended improved performance. None of us likes to be "whacked upside the head" with no clue why. None of us wants to be scolded, reprimanded, criticized, or spanked when we have not been given direction and clarity about what is expected of us. A Conversation for Accountability does not include any of these types of unwanted surprises.

When the punishment or accountability result is viewed by the recipient as worse than the offending action, the recipient understandably thinks he or she is not being heard or respected. This also happens when someone is afraid of the other person. This kind of communication disaster plays out in workplaces when a manager shoots down an idea with an automatic no, without really listening and considering why a proposed idea is not going to be moved forward. Managers are emotionally shut out when they give critical feedback that does not make sense to the employee they are trying to correct.

It is okay to make a mistake. When we are in a culture that really believes this, there is more freedom and less stress. If we

Team member's name _____

1. *Approach*. How will you mentally prepare to address the person?

2. *Describe*. What is the behavior that is unacceptable?

3. *Express*. What are your feelings and thoughts about it?

4. *Suggest*. What new outcomes do you want?

5. *Explain*. What are the benefits to the person of altering his or her behavior?

6. *Ask*. What will you say to ask for a commitment and hold the person accountable?*

think that as a result of making a mistake we will lose something (like our jobs, money, or relationships), we may walk on eggshells. In this case, trust cannot grow. When the punishment is worse than the offense, the message is lost. Victim-like thinking and the blame game emerge. Taking a developmental approach to giving corrective feedback and holding someone accountable is the most effective strategy.

We want to see that we can work through conflict and differences of opinion and belief with others. This is a common crossroads that must be dealt with early in all relationships. How will we correct things with each other? Do you trust that you will be able to talk it out and really listen to each other? If so, you are building the foundation for a solid relationship that can withstand changing conversations, different communication-style preferences, and the ups and downs of normal life.

Early in my career, I worked with the vice president of the IT department of my company. His name was Steve, and he was known to be a screamer. One day he came into my open cube environment screaming my name. Using a High Dominant communication style, Steve boomed so loudly that people poked their heads out of their cubes to see what was going on. He said something like, "Shawn, I cannot believe you let this happen. This was a stupid mistake. How could you be so blind?" The vice president of my department even heard him several offices away. I had no idea what he was talking about. He was accusing me of something I had not done. This was not a private conversation to check in with me on an expected result that we had agreed to; it was public humiliation. This was arbitrary discipline that was not based on fact or agreed-upon accountability.

I was blindsided by this outburst. I made a decision that I would never interact with an employee during the heat of the moment like that. If I could not speak calmly, then I needed to wait until I could. If I could not clearly ask for what I wanted, then I needed to go back to my own office and think it through until I could clearly state my wants and not expect one of my employees to figure it out for me. Have you made a similar commitment to yourself about how you want to interact with people?

People respond differently to stress based on their own preferred communication style. Screamer Steve is a good example of what those with a High Dominant style will do when under stress if they have not learned how to adapt their style. In Conversations for Accountability, it is vital that you understand the other person's communication style and adapt to it so that your message will be heard.

Being in a managerial role is loaded with preconceived ideas for many employees. Some people do not trust managers just because of their title and role. Working through those preconceived ideas openly is important for good management to occur so that healthy Conversations for Accountability emerge in both directions. Being accountable for our commitments may mean we have to give someone else feedback about what he or she is not doing that needs to be done.

I have a commitment about who I want to be as I interact with others. I do not want to squash people. I do want to treat them with dignity and respect, and I also want to be heard and respected. We train people how to interact with us by our Conversations for Accountability with them. I've watched executives scold, belittle, and yell when they do not get what they expected, and I see squashed relationships emerge.

When employees come to me complaining about their work environment and they do not have a request, I sometimes ask them what they really want. Most of the time, a complaint is just an inverted request. If they do not know what they want, I ask them to come back when it is clear for them, or I offer to ask questions to help them gain clarity. It is a crossroads in our communication, but it's important for people to realize nobody will do their thinking for them—they are accountable for deciding what they want. All you can do is help guide them there with a conversation.

Conversations Done Right

Here are some examples of how it sounds when a Conversation for Accountability goes well.

Taylor and Bill

Taylor worked with a man named Bill who would regularly commit to doing something and then not do it. For example, there would be a list of six items that they agreed Bill would be responsible for. Bill would look Taylor in the eye and say he'd complete all the items, and Bill would provide the dates when he would finish each task. That would be the last Taylor would hear from Bill on the topic unless he brought it up to Bill himself. Bill would act annoyed if Taylor brought it up. With a smirk on his face, Bill would say something like "Trust me. I have this covered." And Bill would consistently do several things on the list very well. But Bill would also consistently not do several things on the list at all. Taylor did not know from Bill which items would be done and which ones would not be done.

Taylor decided to point out this pattern to Bill. Taylor initiated the conversation and shared the facts with Bill about what had been happening and why it was breaking trust in their relationship. As a manager needs to, Taylor was clear in his request to be kept up to date on the project status of each item that Bill had committed to completing.

They had this conversation three times over a few months, and in each conversation Taylor gave Bill specific examples of what items had not been completed and noted that Bill had not made Taylor aware that there were problems with delivering on time. Each time Bill promised he would be better at communicating with Taylor about what he agreed to do and would provide interim updates without being annoyed or bitter about having to add this communication step into the process.

A few weeks later, Taylor was back in the same loop with Bill. Taylor did not know what Bill was working on or what would be completed on time. Several tasks fell through the cracks, and Bill seemed nonchalant about it when Taylor brought it up again. Taylor began to see that by enabling this communication pattern with Bill, Taylor was not being accountable himself in regard to his own work as a manager. Taylor realized that his own integrity would be compromised if he continued working with someone he could not trust to get the job done. Taylor explained this to Bill and told him that he had a choice. They could have a daily Conversation for Accountability to keep Bill focused, or Bill could resign.

The outcome was that Bill agreed to learn a new way of managing his commitments. Taylor asked Bill to write down everything he agreed to do and run it by Taylor daily until Taylor was certain that Bill was being accountable for everything he agreed to do. It took several months for Bill to break his bad habits of overcommitting and losing track of what he said he would do, but Taylor stuck it out with Bill by having a daily Conversation for Accountability.

Don and Jamie

If we do not understand communication-style differences as covered in the first part of this book, we may make the wrong assumptions. Each style approaches accountability very differently. High Compliance styles are accountable with data, facts, and logic. High Compliance individuals can be left alone for hours or days with no interaction while they work on a project. In contrast, the High Influence styles are accountable by talking through things in a big-picture manner and interacting in person. High Influencers need in-person communication about progress regularly to keep them focused. High Dominant styles are accountable for the end results and do not want to be monitored on the details. The High Steady styles think about accountability in a step-by-step fashion and want to identify next-action steps daily so they do not get overwhelmed.

Not being aware of these differences created an accountability nightmare for an executive, Don, a chief learning officer at a global company that is a household name. On the first day of his new job, his boss, Jamie, the president of the company, gave Don huge binders with the biographies of employees and asked him to "Get to know every high-potential person at the director level and above in the organization in your first 90 days on the job." This seems clear enough, right?

Don has a natural communication style of an Influencer, and so hearing this excited him. He thought this meant he should get on a plane and go meet face-to-face with each person on the company's high-potential list. The emotion of excitement overtook Don, based on his interpretation of the task at hand. Don was so sure of his new boss's meaning, and so confident due to his communication style, that he didn't bother clarifying whether he was actually supposed to "get to know" the employees in person. Don's boss, Jamie, had a High Compliant communication style. She meant for Don to memorize all the details in these binders so he would know each person's background. She also thought she was clear enough in her request that she did not check in with Don in his first few weeks on the job. She left him to meet with his new team members and to focus on memorizing the data in the binders. Don started flying all over the world meeting executives. At the end of the month, Don gave his expense reports to his assistant to put them into the system.

Can you imagine Jamie's surprise when she realized that Don had gone to meet with over 100 people face-to-face? She was stunned. Jamie could not understand why Don would have done this. She scheduled a meeting with him and realized this was a crossroads conversation. She asked Don, "What made you decide to take all the trips and spend so much money going to meet with each of these people face-to-face?"

Don replied, surprised at her question, "Jamie, you asked me to get to know each person who was on the high-potential list at the director level and above."

Jamie replied, "I meant for you to read their biographies and learn about them from the data I provided you in the succession planning documents."

They both realized they had not asked the question, "How will we hold each other accountable for the desired results? What will it look like when it is done well?" They did not have a plan to check in with each other initially about what was being done.

While this example might surprise you, it shows how senior-level executives have just as many issues with Conversations for Accountability as other managers.

Phrases and Questions to Start a Conversation

Here are some ways to get your Conversation for Accountability started:

- "I'd like to review the goals and where we are with them."
- "What will it look like if this goal is completed well?"
- "How will we hold each other accountable for these goals?"
- "What will be done by the end of the day today?"
- "When will you have this ready for the client?"
- "Do you have time next Tuesday to discuss your goals and what progress has been made against them?"
- "I'm concerned we may have had a misunderstanding, and I'd like to get on the same page with you about what the intention really is."
- "How can I be helpful to you in reaching the agreed-upon deliverable?"
- "How will I know when it has been completed?"
- "Let's establish milestone dates to review the objectives and what we've accomplished thus far."
- "What other tools or resources are needed to ensure your success?"
- "Will you e-mail me when you have finished this so I can move forward with the next part?"
- "Shall we talk every day around 5 p.m. to discuss what was completed that day?"

- "Will you let me know if there is something holding you back from progressing to the next step as soon as you are aware of it so we can think out the options together?"
- "How often would you like me to check in with you to ensure you are on track?"
- "What gets measured gets done. Are we measuring what we want as outcomes?"
- "Is there another way we could approach accountability on this project that we have not yet discussed?"
- *With someone who has read this book or attended the seminar:* "I'd like to have a Conversation for Accountability. When would be a good time for you to do that?"

Mistakes in Conversation

I've observed numerous mistakes in Conversations for Accountability while coaching executives. Some of the most common of these include not agreeing upon goals to be held accountable for, not clearly asking for what you really want, and not giving enough specific detail for the other person to recognize what changes are needed in his or her behavior.

Nina, a manager in a customer service department, told me that she realized that not having rewards or giving acknowledgment when a task is done well would often cause accountability issues. As a new manager, she did not initially tell people when they were doing things well—she expected them to know for themselves. Her team members felt that if no one noticed they were doing well, then why would anyone notice if the task was not done well.

Other sure ways that give rise to accountability problems are to keep blinders on to the fact that deadlines have not been met and to do the work for someone else and not mention it to the person; the problem here is that if you don't point it out when you are doing someone else's work, before too long people will think it is your job. And remember what we discussed about emotional intelligence: When people experience that what they are hearing is criticism, it may trigger fear. Once someone has gone into an emotional state of fear, it will take the person hours to clearly hear what is being said. So set the stage for the conversation productively so that the listener hears the possibility of what is needed clearly and respectfully. The conversation may need to have two or three parts before it really sinks in for the other person.

People who have a preference for the High Influence communication style need to be held accountable verbally. They often need help with goal setting by being asked, "What would be a meaningful goal for you? How would you like to be held accountable in meeting this goal?" Other styles may not realize their need to verbalize this to make it stick for the High Influencer.

When There's No Conversation

The following problems can result when the Conversation for Accountability is missing:

- We teach people that they do not have to respect us.
- We do not model self-respect for those who work with and for us.
- We lose credibility.
- We do not reach the goals that are most meaningful.
- We make excuses that let ourselves off the hook for the results that we'd really prefer to have.

Final Words

Accountability partners can help us keep a goal we might not keep on our own. Once we get the habit in place with our partner, then we are able to keep it going on our own. Look for an accountability buddy who has a successful track record of accomplishment. If you cannot find someone like that, consider hiring a coach who already has extensive expertise in the area in which you want to develop.

When we enable others to disconnect from their commitments or break their word, we are not being accountable to ourselves. Begin to see complaints as inverted requests. When you hear people complain, ask them to describe what they really want. Then suggest that they go ask the right person for what they want. When the punishment is worse than the offense, the message is lost. Victim-like thinking and the blame game emerge.

If we do not understand communication-style differences and use this information to adapt in times of stress, we make assumptions that cause a Conversation for Accountability to fail. When the stakes are high, think about your own style and the style of the people you are working with. How do they need to hear the message in order for it to sink in? What can you do to communicate the message so that they can hear it through their own filters? People with differing communication styles will approach accountability differently.

CHAPTER 11

Conversation for Conflict Resolution

Imagine if someone at IBM had challenged Thomas Watson, the chairman of IBM, in 1943 when he said, "I think there is a world market for maybe five computers." My guess is no one said, "Tom, what if there will be a computer on every desk one day? I know we see this differently, and I am thinking there will be a huge need worldwide for computers. I'd like to discuss this with you because I think we need to be the first to get ourselves ready. Let's identify a project team to explore a strategy around bringing more computers to the marketplace." If we have a corporate culture that does not support conflict resolution, we will not likely have the kind of innovation that brings future wealth. When people are afraid of conflict or differing ideas and do not know how to handle differences of opinions, differences in interpretations of current reality, intuition, and feelings, then innovation does not occur.

Use this conversation when:

- Someone is ignoring an issue that is important to you.
- You notice yourself ignoring an issue that is important to someone who is a stakeholder in your work.

- You need to express differences and disappointments with someone.
- There is chronic tension in a relationship.
- You need to find a path to agreement.
- You want to agree to disagree, without hiding your disagreement and then later acting in a passive aggressive or hostile way.
- You feel anger, bitterness, or resentment.
- You notice someone else is angry, bitter, or resentful.

All about Conflict Resolution

Many people do not allow themselves to see or recognize conflicts in their conversations because they do not know how to identify and resolve conflicts. Fear of past problems that occurred during conflicts has shut down the awareness that a nagging conflict exists. There are several types of conflict:

- Me against myself (a me-me conflict)
- Me against another (a me-you conflict)
- Me caught in the middle between two people against each other (a me-them conflict)
- Me against others within a department or team (a me-team conflict)
- Me against others across several departments or teams (a me–big group conflict)

If we do not admit the issue, we cannot resolve the conflict. Instead we sweep it under the carpet or wear blinders as a symptom of feeling fear, not thinking we can handle a conversation to discuss the conflict and create a resolution. In other words, when the threat of conflict enters the conversation, people often feel fear because they do not know what to do. Their unconscious reaction is to go numb, to lose clarity in their thinking, and to blank out emotionally. Shutting down on the issue, giving in or accepting, complying, submitting passively, acquiescing, or abdicating our own needs—these may be symptoms of what we do when we are unconscious of or unwilling to acknowledge a conflict.

> *The first man to raise a fist is the first man*
> *who ran out of ideas.*
> —H. G. Wells

"What you resist persists" and "Argue for your limitations and they become yours" are helpful sayings in times of conflict. Although I do not know the original sources of either of these, I've been using them for probably 20 years. They have become mantras for me when I realize I am in a conflict. I ask myself, "What am I resisting, and what would it be like if instead I was willing to explore possibilities with curiosity? Can I move into a Conversation for New Possibilities, or am I too attached to arguing for a limitation?"

Holly, a coaching client, was in a deep conflict with her new boss about the vision for the future of the department she had been running for many years. She was deeply resistant to hearing his new ideas. She spent a lot of time in her own head silently fuming with him. She kept dwelling on all the reasons why his ideas would not work, but she never took on the mindset of a learner to explore what his vision would mean. She did not think through the possibilities and ask, "What would happen if we did do this? Then what? Then what would happen next after that?" She did not engage with him in such conversations despite his efforts to talk with her. If she had done so, she would have seen new possibilities for herself and would have understood that he had her slotted for a much bigger role. Because she would not stop resisting him, she hung onto her limitations about the way the department had to work. One day, as a result of a conversation with a close colleague, she realized that her resistance was creating more conflict than was necessary. She was then able to shift her own energy and approach a conversation with her boss, willing to really hear his ideas with an open mind.

145

Employees and bosses who find a way honestly and respectfully to hear each other's ideas and to share their opinions when they do not agree are the ones who create strong relationships that are meaningful. But it takes two people to do this; the boss cannot do it alone. Nor can an employee create this type of relationship with a boss who is not willing to listen and engage in the dialogue. It is how you work through conflict together that matters most to this important relationship.

Conversation for Conflict Resolution works best when neither party approaches the dialogue with a focus on proving the other party wrong or trying to get everyone to see that his or her own idea is the only right one. It is useful to reframe a conflict to see the possibility for creating something better that can come from working through a disagreement. Conflict does not have to result in a fight. It can create a healthy discussion of differences in needs and wants. When we learn how to listen respectfully to each other, the face of conflict changes—it no longer leads to fights. Instead it leads to engaged solutions-focused thinking on everyone's part. Many wonderful experiences and products were born out of recognizing differences in needs, identifying unmet needs, and working through the conflict. Slowing down when faced with conflict helps some people to stay aware and not go into autopilot fear or anger.

Conscious and Unconscious Conflict

No doubt you've experienced both conscious conflict and unconscious conflict. An example of a conscious conflict would be one I helped work through with a client recently. This was the scene when I was invited into the discussion:

Craig wanted the new vice president of sales to be located in Chicago. Dan wanted the new vice president of sales to be located in San Francisco. Both Craig and Dan shared their desires openly with each other while I was in the room. This led to a meaningful conversation in which they really listened to each other's needs and the pros and cons of each option. I engaged each of them in a dialogue about where the business was going so they could share their current view of reality and the future vision. Such a conflict can lead to feelings of anger or fear if the participants do not listen fully to each other, and so part of what I do in facilitating is to make sure they stay present in the conversation. The discussion could also lead to a power play by one of them if they do not have mutual respect and try to work through the conversation together. We had three conversations over several days until there was a decision they both could accept. It was not about one of them winning and the other losing; they both won because they really heard each other and made a decision together.

With unconscious conflict there is a passive avoidance of the issue. Many years ago when I was in an unhealthy professional relationship with a man named Ed, I often did not address the real issue directly with him because I was afraid doing so would escalate into a fight. It did not feel like there was room to have a meaningful conversation where we really listened to each other. I did not think he would hear me. So what I did instead was take the pictures of us, photos that had been taken for the company magazine and at conferences where we were guest speakers, off the wall in my office; and I would put them away for a few days. Eventually, I would sweep the issue under the proverbial carpet and then hang the pictures back on the wall. I got to the point where I did not see the conflict between us at all, but I'd realize I was once again thinking about removing the pictures of us together from view. I now call this type of unconscious conflict "taking the pictures off the wall," because that was the symptom that enabled me to realize and admit when I was in deep conflict about something with Ed. This is now a sign that a Conversation for Conflict Resolution is needed.

I had to let myself acknowledge the conflict before I could address it. To do this, we typically need to force ourselves out of our comfort zone. Fear, including stuffed-down anger that has turned into fear, is the emotion underlying this unconscious behavior; and how this type of fear shows up in our thinking and physical being is different for all of us. My unconscious fear reaction of taking the pictures off the wall may sound very strange to you, but I assure you that most people who feel fear have things they unconsciously do that would be illogical to someone else.

As I wrote in Chapter 1 on emotional intelligence, when people fight about something, the subject of the argument is rarely the real issue. The real issue is about feelings of vulnerability, connectedness, safety, trust, or love—which are all emotional states. Ask yourself, what is the emotional state that is driving the conflict? Fear and anger are usually involved. People are angry that they are not being heard and acknowledged. Their boundaries have been crossed, and they are not being heard as they try to voice their needs. Others are afraid that they are losing something that impacts their status, family, money, and self-concept. Uncover and acknowledge the emotional reasons for the conflict, and you will be better able to create a resolution.

Conversations Done Right

Here are some examples of how it sounds when a Conversation for Conflict Resolution goes well.

Amit and Rishi

Amit and Rishi have been equal partners for several years in an architecture firm. Amit likes to manage the company finances, and Rishi has been willing to let him do so. Amit has high utilitarian and theoretical values and a High Compliance and Dominant communication style. Rishi has high aesthetic and theoretical values and a High Influence and Steady communication style. Every few months, Amit provides Rishi with an overview of the finances in an update meeting that Rishi seems to take for granted, assuming that all is handled well by Amit and the bookkeepers. Recently their receivables have been less than usual, and Amit has realized they will need to make some changes to their monthly expenses. Amit has asked Rishi to meet to discuss this several times, and Rishi has uncharacteristically missed the meetings that were on the schedule for this financial discussion.

As he is driving home, Amit thinks about how he and Rishi are supposed to be equal partners, but he seems to be the only one worrying about how to handle this mess they are in. Amit examines his own feelings and acknowledges he is covering up anger and an internal conflict that he needs to discuss. He's feeling dumped on, and he does not know how to solve this situation himself. It is clear they need more business, but they have to make some decisions fast about what expenses to cut until they bring in new business.

Now that Amit sees this clearly, he calls Rishi at home that evening. He intentionally uses language that matches Rishi's preferred communication style by casually saying, "Rishi, I need your help. Would this be a good time to talk through what is on my mind so we can be on the same page together about how we handle our business finances?"

Rishi agrees that he can make time now for this conversation. So Amit continues, "Rishi, we've been very lucky in our business over the past several years because we had some large long-term contracts that kept the revenue coming in. In the past few months those contracts have ended, and we do not have a strong enough pipeline of new projects coming into the business for us to pay our existing monthly bills and the staff. We need to decide what we want to cut."

Rishi is a wonderful architect and has designed award-winning buildings, but he really struggles with the fundamentals of finances and the importance of getting every bill paid on time, which is core to Amit's values. Rishi notices that he does not want to deal with this issue. He'd just prefer Amit handle it. Rishi says, "Amit, I trust you to make recommendations about what is the best thing for us to do now. What do you propose?"

Amit replies, "I am so stressed over this because if we lay off some of our staff, we may not be able to take on a larger project a few months from now because we'll lose them. There are pros and cons with each option, and I can't see clearly enough which is the best way for us to go. But if we do not cut something, we are going to go under as a business. Or we could try to get a loan, but I do not know if we could get financing in the current economy and with our pipeline being what it is now. We are stuck, Rishi, and I do not know what to recommend. What I really want is for us to be partners in this and make the decisions together. I want your voice in this too."

There is a long silence. Rishi finally breaks the silence and says, "What if we went to talk with a business financial advisor to get an expert's advice? Would that help to alleviate your stress, knowing we are going to get help, Amit?" This question from Rishi causes a rush of anger in Amit; he thinks to himself, "Rishi why aren't you hearing me. This is not just my issue—it is *our* issue; it's not just my stress—it should be *our* stress." Amit remembers to self-regulate and that anger is a signal that his boundaries have been crossed. Amit asks himself, "How can I explain my boundaries so that Rishi hears me?"

Amit replies, "Yes, I am willing to do that. However, we are not going to be able to make payroll next month, so we have to do this quickly. Rishi, I also think it would be helpful for you and me to sit down with the current expenses in front of us and go through each category to see where we can cut together. For example, each of us in the company has a paid radio subscription that adds up to over a thousand dollars. We could quickly cut that, but I do not want to make that decision by myself unless you are willing to stand behind me and agree to it." That got through to him. Rishi loves his XM radio and says he is initially unwilling to let it go until he sees all the expenses. They agree to meet early the next morning in the office.

The next morning, Amit is prepared with all the summary expenses in a spreadsheet. He hands it to Rishi and says, "How about if each of us looks at where we would make our first $15,000 worth of cuts. We can discuss that to see where we need to go from there."

After several rounds on the spreadsheet and lots of sighs, Rishi says, "Amit, I'm willing to forgo my draw from the business for a couple of months while we find new clients. I had not realized the situation we were in, and I see clearly now why you have been on edge about this. We will make these decisions together." It takes a few moments for Rishi's words to sink in for Amit. Now Amit feels like they are on the same page looking together at the same problem.

Once Amit felt like they were working together on the decision-making process, the conflict and the stress toward his partner lessened for him. Within a few days they made major decisions about where to cut their expenses, including their XM radio subscriptions. They are both continuing to learn about running the finances of a small business. They decided to look at this problem as their "Financial Adventure" and take it on together.

Tina and Karl

Tina, a coaching client who is working on learning stronger negotiation skills, wants to buy a new car. Her husband and business partner, Karl, wants to keep the car they have for two more years while they continue to invest in the business. Tina realizes they do not want the same thing in this situation. She brings this up to discuss the pros and cons of each option openly, and together they acknowledge that they differ in their wants. Ultimately she asks, "What values do we have that impact this decision?" It turns out they have a history of buying what they want with cash on hand. They do not want to borrow money for this type of purchase. Tina and Karl let that shared value be the deciding factor for purchasing the car. When will they have enough saved to pay for it with cash on hand? The answer to this values question is the resolution to the conflict. This creates a resolution they can both live with. It is solution focused and enables them both to feel like a win-win outcome was created.

Phrases and Questions to Start a Conversation

Here are some ways to get your Conversation for Conflict Resolution started:

- "I'd like to hear more about your perspective and feelings. Would you be willing to share more so I can better understand your perspective?"
- "We may see things differently here, and I'd like to explore what we agree on as well as where we are viewing things differently. Would you be willing to start with where we have agreement?"
- "Sometimes it is useful to agree to disagree and move on. Are we in one of those situations? Are we both able to move on and let this go so it is not preventing us from doing the next action?"
- "I'd like to invite you to have coffee off-site sometime next week. I am struggling with something, and I would really appreciate the opportunity to discuss it with you to get your input."
- "I have a commitment to focus on the desired behavior and outcomes we'd like to create rather than focus on what we don't want. Will you join me in this?"
- "What would you need for us to work through this issue?"
- "What are the values underlying your needs in this situation?"
- "Is there something we are tiptoeing around that we would both benefit by discussing?"
- "I'm conflicted about an issue, and I'd like to talk it out with someone who is unbiased, who will ask me questions to get me thinking in new ways. Will you be that person?"

Mistakes in Conversations

Over the years, I've observed numerous mistakes in Conversation for Conflict Resolution. One cluster of mistakes involves consciously or unconsciously avoiding the conflict entirely.

Some people consciously ignore the fact that they're feeling fear and make everything look fine by stuffing it down inside. Others do not realize that avoidance and silence cannot cure conflict, and so they ignore a conflict in the hopes that it might go away. But if you have had three or more instances of thinking about the conflict and it troubles you, then you need to do something to address it.

As a case in point, this is what can happen when you *don't* address conflict: Bob does not allow conflict to be expressed. As a result, not much changes. He does not experience significant improvements because he's not willing to let the heat bubble up in discussions. He is afraid his team members will disagree with him or each other, and he does not know how to handle it when this happens. If a conflict begins in a meeting, he will say something like "Let's take that offline and leave it for another meeting with just the two of you." Then no one ever follows up on the issue since Bob would be needed to help work things through.

Mistakes that are made during a Conversation for Conflict Resolution include dismissing or not listening to issues that someone wants to express. Often the person not being heard is on your team or is a stakeholder to your work. Another common mistake is for people not to ask for what they want and instead wait for other parties to say what they want.

Some people do an emotional tap dance on eggshells around an issue and do not speak clearly about what the real issue is. On the other hand, some resort to screaming and bullying. And others make sarcastic or snide comments that indirectly point at the issue. A close cousin to this latter behavior is to hold in hostile remarks only to have them come out sideways later as cheap shots or sarcastic remarks. You might be surprised to know that some people can do these things without being aware that they are doing so. Some of us simply don't realize that we may be coming from our worst behavior when we are in a conflict. If we do not know how this shows up to others, we may be sabotaging our ability to create a meaningful solution.

A lack of awareness of communication styles also poses problems. A successful conversation would be very difficult to have if we don't bear in mind that each of the communication styles handles conflict differently.

When There's No Conversation

The following problems can result when the Conversation for Conflict Resolution is missing:

- People lose respect for their managers, peers, and colleagues.
- The organization has lost a valuable means to solve problems and take on issues that could help the organization grow.
- Hard feelings persist and turn into resentment thereby diminishing the likelihood of reaching goals.
- Teams stay in the "forming" stage and are not able to move to a high-performing level.

Final Words

If we do not admit there is an issue, we cannot resolve a conflict. If we take on the mindset of someone who is on an exploration to learn and seek out new ways of viewing things, then we will be open to exploring possibilities to resolve conflicts. Being in a conflict does not necessarily mean that a fight is occurring or is obvious to others. Many useful products and services were born out of recognizing differences in needs, discussing the unmet needs, and working through the underlying conflict to resolve the issues. If we are not stepping up to deal with unresolved conflict on the teams we lead, the team members will begin to lose respect for our management capabilities. Respect from others often comes once they have seen we are willing to deal with conflict in productive ways.

When we are too passive in avoiding an issue, it would be helpful to look under that behavior at what the feeling is. Often we will discover that fear is holding us back from speaking up about what we need to discuss. Forcing ourselves out of a comfort zone may help us to notice conflicts and speak up about them in ways that lead to a better outcome and a solution.

The most successful conflict facilitators understand the other side's concerns and needs as much as they understand their own. They ask questions and deeply listen so that the other side sees the open willingness to be in a mutual exploration and problem-solving dialogue. It is debilitating to be filled with anger and fear from unacknowledged conflict or conflict that is habitually ignored. Although we cannot make others change when they are not willing to, we can invite them to explore what the impact is in seeing new possibilities, even if they are resistant to do so.

When people are trying to end a conflict or injustice they feel they are suffering, they need to deeply understand the other party too. If they do not do this, they are focusing on themselves and not the real issue. This is what creates victim-like circular thinking. If you feel you are stuck in a no-win situation, it is worth looking at your own circular thinking that is creating the victim pattern. Seek out role models who have worked through conflict successfully. Be open to their observation and feedback about your thinking and what you could change to create a solution.

CHAPTER 12

Conversation for Breakdown

Sometimes one type of conversation leads us into another type naturally. If a Conversation for Conflict Resolution does not produce results, and it seems as though we've tried just about everything, then we need to acknowledge the severity of the conflict and move on, rather than wallowing. A breakdown occurs when things are not working and we are in an oscillating pattern. Acknowledging the breakdown is the first step. Just admitting to yourself that you are in a breakdown around an issue can cause you to let go of the resistance and trigger a move into a new conversation.

Use this conversation when:

- You feel jammed up, stuck, afraid, and unable to think clearly.
- You notice yourself or someone else caught in circular thinking that is not creating what is needed next.
- A person or team is not meeting its goals.
- You are admitting you do not know what to do next.
- You are ready to move through the stuck places.

All about Breakdown

When we admit that we are experiencing a breakdown in getting to our goals, we free ourselves to reevaluate what the options are. Persistence is useful, but not if we are persistent in an oscillating pattern. In Chapter 10 on Conversations for Accountability, I shared an example of Tim, who was struggling in his interpersonal relationships. Tim had to admit to himself that he was in a breakdown in his ability to build professional relationships before he was willing to explore new ways of interacting with others. This included coaching Tim to see for himself that the issue was not his manager's problem; it was his lack of empathy in interpersonal communication that was the breakdown. For a few days Tim was withdrawn and hurt, and it was during this time that I was able to talk with him to have him see that a Conversation for Breakdown could be useful to launch him in a new direction.

> *Life's challenges are not supposed to paralyze you;*
> *they're supposed to help you discover who you are.*
> —Bernice Johnson Reagon

If we talk with the people who crossed our boundaries and ask for what we want, we may be able to clear up the issue. However, sometimes the people we talk to do not hear us; rather they become quite defensive and shut down our request completely. When our boundaries are repeatedly ignored, bitterness and resentment are sure to follow. What do we do when we get to that point? Sometimes we need to move into a conversation to withdraw and disengage; albeit, it may be difficult to get there because the person with whom we have the issue is core in our lives or business and shows up over and over.

One of my mentors, Justice, shared with me that this is something he wrestled with for many years. He told me that his initial response to a breakdown was avoidance. He just ignored whatever and whoever caused him to be repeatedly angry. He realized the problem with this approach is that the anger is not dealt with—it's merely suppressed, and it invariably rears its ugly head later again and again. So Justice tried a forgiveness approach to deal with being stuck in anger. He learned this is not a pragmatic solution either, because it is one-sided or often confused with acting as if it did not happen. This is also not very practical long term when we are required to interact with the person or people who are part of the breakdown. The best approach is working through the breakdown by getting clear on what would cause momentum.

Momentum versus Oscillation

What is momentum? Imagine getting in a car you enjoy driving, intending to reach a desired destination. You have all you need to get where you want to go: directions, gas, money, and snacks for the trip. All goes well, and you arrive at your destination just as you planned. This is momentum.

You've probably experienced momentum in building relationships and working on projects where you achieve your desired results. I have a client who has created great momentum in bringing the right salespeople into his organization. For this client, we built a screening process and an initial training program that gets people up to speed in three months, whereas it used to take six months to a year. This is another example of momentum.

What is oscillation? Imagine sitting in a rocking chair, moving back and forth, thinking you are in a car going to a desired destination without really moving forward at all. This is an oscillating pattern. Symptoms of oscillation are feeling frustration, engaging in the "blame game," or having the same conversation with someone several times as if it has not been discussed before. Oscillating patterns can lead to a Conversation for Breakdown.

Oscillation was the foundation of a professional relationship I had with a man named Rick. I kept thinking that the relationship was going to yield meaningful results. We'd take a few steps toward working together. I'd share my ideas and connections with him. He would make promises about what he'd do, but ultimately I would not receive anything in return. He'd ask for more from me, and I would deliver. He either wanted to talk to more people or wanted more information but never gave anything of himself to the possible project. Repeatedly and with excitement he would say he wanted to work together and co-create, but nothing followed that. This is an oscillating structure. Signals that we were oscillating were my feelings of resentment, frustration, and bitterness. Nowadays, the moment I begin to have those emotional symptoms, I see it clearly and ask for what is needed to move things forward.

All of us have a "click-whirl" trigger in our minds that sets up the foundation for momentum building or for oscillation. Most of us are unaware of the patterns we've created. We just know the results after the fact: either we ended up in our desired destination, or we did not. Learning to see the signs along the way will prevent us from investing lots of time in an oscillating pattern that leads to breakdown.

With professional teams, I regularly ask myself the question, "Where would momentum take us next?" The answer gives me direction about what to initiate. Sometimes it's making time to talk about the current reality or the progress we've made recently and inviting team members to identify where they want to go next. Keeping our focus on momentum and growth keeps team members engaged.

Knowing how to recognize your momentum pattern versus your oscillation pattern will enable you to stop the oscillation with someone before investing years trying to figure out what's not working. Perhaps you've stayed in professional relationships or jobs that were built on oscillating patterns. We don't remove ourselves from oscillating patterns soon enough because we fail to observe the foundation as it is being built. With experience, though, we can learn how to construct everything we do with our momentum pattern, which, in turn, creates ongoing success.

When we realize we are in an oscillating pattern, it's time to acknowledge a breakdown and change the conversation.

Three Steps to Dealing with a Breakdown

After 20 years of talking to dozens of amazing people who lived through significant breakdowns, reading books by experts on this topic, and trying all kinds of approaches, I have found what I think to be the best approach to this type of breakdown. The approach boils down to these three steps:

1. Ask yourself what about the situation could be a lesson? What is the learning from this experience? How did you get into this situation? What could you take out of this situation that could be of great value to you and then to others? This is self-reflection done privately.
2. Next, commit to never putting yourself in that situation again. Do everything that is in your power to avoid repeating the circumstances that created the breakdown.
3. And finally, most importantly, reach out to help others so they do not make the same mistake. Find a way to use the learned lesson to help yourself, and others, in your work and personal life by finding a positive use for the experience. Find a silver lining, and share it with others. This enables any residual resentment or bitterness to go away.

By applying these steps to a breakdown that involves anger, bitterness, and resentment, you will find *stunning* relief. It does not change the fact that it happened, but it turns it into something that benefits you and others.

Conversations Done Right

Here are some examples of how it sounds when a Conversation for Breakdown goes well.

Laura

Laura wanted a promotion to partner in the law firm where she worked. She had requested this several times and felt she was not getting anywhere. She began to feel angry at the firm and partners. She decided to admit she was in a breakdown about meeting her goal using the strategy she had. She did not know what step to take next. She asked several people in other law firms to recount to her the sequence that enabled them to move into a partner role and describe how they made the transition to partner. This enabled her to come at it from a very different direction and helped her to create a different approach. She created a Conversation for Creating New Possibilities with several of the partners and outlined for them several options she saw for herself. She asked them to help her think out what would happen if she accomplished each option. Then she took it to the next step and asked what would happen after that and then after that. This ultimately led her to being offered a partner role within two months. She now mentors young lawyers about how to identify the steps to becoming a partner and helps them evaluate if that is what they really want for themselves.

Brian

Brian wanted to buy a new business that he thought would fit nicely with the one he already owned. For several months he was in a due diligence process with a company he was very excited about buying. He began to notice that the owner of the business he wanted to buy seemed to be stalling on selling. Then the owner told Brian that he had showed his offer to others, and as a result he'd gotten an offer that was three times the amount Brian had offered. Brian felt angry and then bitter about what was happening. He learned that in the early stages of exploring to purchase a new business it is wise to create an Intent to Purchase agreement that prevents the owner from sharing the details of an offer with others. The owner asked Brian to match the new offer. Brian did not know what to do.

Brian and I had a conversation during which he admitted to himself that this was a breakdown in reaching his goal, and he realized he did not want to move forward with this person. He felt trust had been broken. He withdrew his offer and decided to stop striving to purchase this company. He wrote out what he learned from the situation and what he would do differently next time to avoid the problem. He drew up an Intent to Purchase agreement that he could use in the future. A month later he began to look at other options. Within a few weeks he found another business to purchase that was a much better fit for him. He applied what he learned about setting up the conversation to purchase the business, and this sale went through seamlessly. A year later he shared what he learned from this experience in a presentation to a group of entrepreneurs.

Brian told me that admitting there was a breakdown caused him to step back and not get caught up in forcing it to happen. This also gave him a better perspective on what his real needs were.

Kate and Jason

Kate led a team of technical support professionals with extensive knowledge of the complex software their company regularly won awards for supporting. Kate was very proud of the team and its accomplishments. Kate's boss, the owner of the company, was also proud of this industry-acknowledged team. However, Kate had a problem: one of the most senior members of her team, Jason, hoarded information.

Jason's hoarding of information meant that he did not teach others what he knew. He loved being the most knowledgeable person in the department in his area of expertise, and so when someone came to ask him to help with a complex problem, Jason would solve the problem but not share how he did it. Kate realized that Jason's knowledge level was exclusive to him, and this was dangerous for a company their size. The team needed at least two or three additional people who could re-create what

Jason did if Jason was out of the office. The company's service-level agreements would be severely compromised if something happened; and as it was, Jason chose to work late nights when he was on vacation just so he would not have to teach someone to cover for him while he was out.

Kate had discussed this issue with Jason several times, and nothing changed. She made it very clear in her performance discussions with him that she wanted him to share his know-how with two specific people so that she did not feel as if she were held hostage by his exclusive knowledge. She'd asked more times than she wanted to, and nothing had happened. Jason ignored her requests, knowing his special skills gave him the upper hand. She could not fire him for not doing as she asked because he was the only person in the company who knew how to do what he did and his expertise was vital to operations of their department. Her inability to handle the situation made her angry. Of course, anger is a sign that something or someone has crossed your boundaries. It is a signal that we need to clean up the boundary violation. Ignoring our own emotions will lead to breakdown. Kate was feeling this regularly as it related to her relationship with Jason.

Kate began to realize she was in a breakdown.

Initially Kate decided to ignore Jason's disregard for her request. In fact, she would not walk down the hallway where his office was located; she would walk around the long way just so she would not have to see his space. She decided to hire two additional people and gave them the assignment to learn as much as they could from Jason. She had them report to him even though it was well known that he did not manage people well because he would not teach them. She informed them that this would be a six-month arrangement for them to learn as much as they could.

Kate admitted to herself that she was not being true to her own management beliefs because she had created an exclusive status category for Jason that negatively impacted others in the department. She was in this breakdown with him way too long, and it was impacting her credibility as a manager with her staff and her own boss. Jason was not just a hoarder of information in his head, as is typical of this type of hoarding; he also had piles of resource books, computers, and manuals cluttering his office so that there was no space for anyone to walk into his office. Every surface was covered with computers or stacked high with material. He used his stacks as his primary reason why he did not have the time to teach others what he knew. Jason's office space was an embarrassment to the organization because it needed to be cleaned and organized—our space is a reflection of what is going on in our mind and our energy.

After getting agreement from her boss to move in this direction, Kate put Jason on a performance plan. She explained to him that he would be fired within 30 days if his office was not cleaned and organized so that he could then make the time to prioritize what he knew and share it. She hired a professional organizer to coach Jason and told both of them this was a make-or-break deal for his career with the company. Jason cleaned his office and learned new organizing skills that enabled him to pull out what was most important to train several people so that he was not a bottleneck in the department.

If Kate had not confronted Jason and had stayed stuck in the breakdown, neither of them would have grown from the experience.

Phrases and Questions to Start a Conversation

Here are some ways to get your Conversation for Breakdown started:

- "It seems to me like we are stuck. Do you see it that way too?"
- "We have a commitment to do . . . , but we have not been able to move in that direction. What is it that is keeping us from moving forward?"

- "If someone else were looking at this situation, would that person say that I am (or we are) oscillating instead of moving forward?"
- "Is it possible for me to put this all in the drawer for a few hours and step away from it, perhaps go for a long walk, visit with a friend, or take a hot bath, and then revisit this situation determined to get unstuck with clarity about what I want to do next?"
- "At this rate, we will not be able to make payroll next week. What do we want to do about this?"
- "Let's take 24 hours to think this through and determine whether we should move forward with this decision."
- "It seems to me we are in need of a conversation to acknowledge our breakdown. Do you agree?"

Mistakes in Conversation

Not admitting we are in a breakdown is common. Sometimes someone has to hold a mirror up for us to see it clearly. If someone approaches you to express concern that there is a breakdown, listen carefully rather than go into a defensive position.

Be sure to get input from key stakeholders. They might have insight that you do not have. Leaving stakeholders out of the process can lead to creating a structure that has gaps in it. Think through the steps very clearly. If you leave the "how" up to other people, you may end up with a very different result than anticipated. If we do not admit to ourselves that we are in a breakdown and are stuck in oscillation, we may stay there way too long. We may work for a boss or a company that is not fulfilling and is a compromise to our own values.

When There's No Conversation
The following problems can result when the Conversation for Breakdown is missing:

- Keeping blinders on
- Complaining
- Gossip
- A lack of cooperation
- Martyr-like behavior
- Bitterness and resentment

Final Words

If a Conversation for Accountability does not produce results, then we need to acknowledge the conflict and the breakdown. Ignoring our own emotions or the emotions of those we work with will lead to a shutdown autopilot state. You do not have to stay stuck in anger, bitterness, and resentment.

The lack of momentum creates oscillation that is frustrating and often results in the blame game. It also causes us to feel like we are having the same old conversation over and over again. When this happens, ask, "Where would momentum take us next?" The answer to this question will give you insights about what actions to take next. When we recognize we are in an oscillating pattern, it is time to acknowledge a breakdown and change the conversation that is creating the circular thinking.

CHAPTER 13

Conversation for Withdrawal and Disengagement

Not all relationships need to go forward. Sometimes, when things just are not working out, we have to take a step back and disengage from a job, friend, colleague, or business partner. When we realize this is the case, how can we end on a healthy, respectful note?

Use this conversation when:

- You realize a relationship is a no-win situation for anyone.
- There is nothing you can do to help or support a team member or situation in moving forward with its current goals.
- You are stuck in a pattern of anger, sadness, or fear with a boss, team, or group.
- It is time to move on.
- You recognize when a conversation or relationship does not need to move forward.
- It's time to admit a relationship is toxic.
- You realize you need to let go when the other party is not letting go (he or she is clinging on out of fear and neediness, and it is not healthy for either of you).

All about Withdrawal and Disengagement

We are living in a time of great change. Many people have experienced losing their jobs over the past year. During this time, they realized they would be changing their day-to-day reality of going into their offices or following their normal routines, and many Conversations for Withdrawal and Disengagement occurred. Ending a relationship, project, or daily routine triggers Conversations for Withdrawal and Disengagement.

Suzanne, the president of a well-respected retained search firm, shared with me that she receives e-mails and phone calls from would-be job candidates who would like her to connect them to someone she knows. Due to the dramatic change in the unemployment rate, the volume of the e-mails and calls for Suzanne has been overwhelming. These job searchers can see in Suzanne's LinkedIn profile that she knows executives at companies where they would like to work. The phone conversation or e-mail is usually a solicitation for Suzanne to forward the attached résumé on to one of her professional connections. Suzanne has learned the hard way that such a conversation is a no-win situation for her. If she forwards the résumé of a person she does not know, she risks tarnishing her credibility with a client she knows well. If she spends time getting to know the person looking for a job in an area she is not currently retained for, there is nothing she can do to help. Suzanne has learned to withdraw from such situations by sending the person who is making the request an article on how to prepare for interviews and meet people who are hiring. She wishes the person well and does not initiate any follow-up.

Sometimes we realize it is time to end a relationship, but the other person does not want to stop the communication. One of my clients, Frank, decided that he no longer wanted to be part of communication that is focused on gossip. His colleague Sally, on the other hand, does nothing but gossip. Sally has no desire to change this bad habit in conversations; in fact she does not even seem to be aware that she is gossiping. Frank decided to withdraw from these types of conversations with Sally by addressing the problem head-on. "Sally," he said, "I'd rather that we not talk about people who are not in the room with us." He had to say this several times over three separate conversations before it really sank in for Sally that Frank meant what he was saying—that he would withdraw rather than join in that type of conversation—and she stopped gossiping.

It is unrealistic to think that all relationships will be enjoyable or friendly forever. Business and personal relationships can deteriorate for a wide variety of reasons that revolve around loss of trust, integrity, and respect. Sometimes we need to admit to ourselves that we are in a toxic or one-sided relationship that is causing more problems than it is worth. In this case it is best to end the connection so that we can invest our time in relationships that are meaningful and enjoyable.

If you have to call into question whether or not a relationship is one-sided or toxic, it probably is. If you are permanently shut down around someone and feel uncomfortable in the person's presence no matter what you do to improve the situation, you are likely in a toxic relationship. It's time to make a change. Physical and emotional abuses are *automatic* walk-away signs. If someone verbally abuses you in the office, it will just as likely happen again. It is a long road to repair a relationship that has suffered from verbal abuse, and it is not always worth the emotional investment to work on it. Before ending a connection, though, it is worthwhile to ask several questions to avoid repeating the same pattern:

* How did this situation come to be?
* What was my part in the deterioration of this connection?
* What were the early signs that something was off, and how did I respond to them?

It's important to remain as nonjudgmental as possible by objectively looking at the answers from your own viewpoint as well as the other person's. If the person is a colleague or a

171

business contact that you will have to remain in touch with in one form or another, it is worth it to explore some form of facilitated discussion to work through the issues to see if a resolution can be created before ending the relationship.

Many years ago, Tim decided to leave an organization in which he had been a partner for 10 years. He realized that his work was not meeting his own needs even though none of the other partners had done anything wrong. He wanted to end the partnership, and the others did not. Tim worked with me as a coach to help him articulate to the other partners why leaving the partnership was the best option for all of them. He explained what his core values were and how they differed from the mission of the firm. He helped the other partners to understand their own values motivators and how they were not aligned with his. Once it became clear that there was a fundamental misalignment in values between them, it became clear that a Conversation for Withdrawal and Disengagement was required. The partners were then able to create a healthy closure with no bitterness on anyone's part. Now they are able to amicably attend professional and social events and enjoy one another's company.

It is important to accept that you do not owe someone else a long, drawn-out explanation about why you want to end the connection if the person you want to move away from has severely crossed your boundaries. You are not responsible for the other person's growth or development, and the other person is not likely to hear you even if you try to help. Creating a detailed development plan for the other party will only keep you stuck in a breakdown.

When Someone Withdraws from You

About a year ago, someone I'd known for 10 years and whom I deeply respect told me she no longer wanted me as a client. That's right; someone began a Conversation for Withdrawal and Disengagement with *me*. She went on to explain that when I called her, I never seemed to ask if she wanted to help me. Instead I usually just dictated what I wanted her to do in an "overly familiar, bossy tone." This pattern offended her so deeply that she ended our connection via a phone conversation.

I realized she had every right to end the client relationship. In the moment the conversation took place, it hurt. I valued her very much, and she apparently did not feel the same for me. I accepted her stand and the fact that this disengagement was what she needed for her own self-respect.

I decided that the most positive outcome would be to use this conversation to grow from the experience. I asked her if she would provide me a few examples of what had happened so that I would not make that same mistake again with others. She was kind enough to do so via e-mail. We have not spoken since, and I respect her for communicating that our relationship was over. Now I heed the lesson I learned from this person, and I ask my clients more questions rather than assuming that because we've worked together for a long time that they still want to continue working together.

The above example is one of different values and different communication styles taking their toll in the long run. She had adapted her style to mine for too long and no longer wanted to have to make the adaptation. Had I realized this, I would have been willing to adapt my style to work with her. Because she did not create a conversation to discuss that possibility, we both missed out now. Walking away can be the best and most respectful choice if it doesn't seem worth it to invest the time and emotional energy into working through the issues.

Conversations Done Right

Here are some examples of how it sounds when a Conversation for Withdrawal and Disengagement goes well.

Joe and Lauren

After a year of working with Lauren as his business attorney, Joe acknowledged to himself that she was making things more complicated than they needed to be. This was likely happening as a result of her own fears and was a way to increase her hours and thus her bill. Joe ignored this at first because he did not want to burn a bridge with her. Then he decided to compare her approach to another attorney's method of handling a situation. After making this comparison, it was clear Lauren was taking significantly longer and turning over issues that did not need to be dealt with at that time. Joe decided he did not want to continue working with her. He concluded it was time to close the relationship with a Conversation for Withdrawal and Disengagement.

"Lauren," he said, "we've decided to move forward with another attorney for our business at this time. Perhaps sometime in the future we will need your assistance again, so I'd like to keep the door open in the event we need your help and you are available at that time."

Lauren was caught off guard. She demanded to know what was wrong with their business relationship. As her client, Joe did not think it was his responsibility to educate her on how her fear appeared to be causing her to make things much more complicated than they needed to be. He simply said, "Lauren, I appreciate your help, but I've simply decided to use someone else for other areas in the future, as I think it plays to his strengths and area of expertise. Thank you very much for your help." In many cases, such as when dealing with a client or peer, it may not be a good idea to get into the nitty-gritty of exactly what went wrong, or you may not want to expend much energy in explaining what is totally clear to you. This leads to one of the other types of conversations.

Sharon

Sharon Lundy is a manager at a luxury retail store. She recently decided to end her connection with someone who worked for another retail firm whom she deeply respected as a professional colleague for many years. Sharon realized the relationship had been one-sided for a long time. She was always the one giving, offering, sharing ideas and information, and he was taking but not giving back. Three things happened back-to-back with him that caused her to see this pattern clearly. She made the decision to stop communicating with him. She said she was withdrawing from their connection for a while. He told her he did not understand why she made this decision. She realized it was not her responsibility to teach him how to be a giving professional friend or how to maintain a friendship. He is a taker, and that is not her responsibility to resolve for him. She accepted that she did not need to explain or justify her decision to end the relationship because it was causing her more annoyance than it was worth. Self-respect in this case is to learn the lesson and move on.

Phrases and Questions to Start a Conversation

Here are some ways to get your Conversation for Withdrawal and Disengagement started:

- "Thank you for the opportunity to work with you. I've learned so much while I was here. It is now time for me to move on and continue my learning, though."
- "This is no longer working for me, and I've decided to make a change for myself. It is not a move against you; it is a step ahead for me."
- "I have another opportunity that I want to explore at this time."
- "This role no longer fits with my vision and values for my career. As a result, I need to make a change for myself."
- "I've decided I need to make some changes for myself. My changes have an impact on you and our working relationship, so I wanted to make you aware of what I am doing."
- "I am choosing to narrow my client list to my top three clients. Unfortunately that means I'd like to transition our work over to another person."

Mistakes in Conversation

We know by how we feel that we are in a relationship that is toxic. Be alert to the signals, and recognize that it is likely time to withdraw and disengage. Prolonging the conversation can cause us to stay so long in this relationship that we lose our own self-respect and confidence. Furthermore, when having a conversation, we can be polite, but we do not owe others an explanation for our decision, nor do we need their permission to disengage—that does not have to be part of the conversation.

When There's No Conversation

The following problems can result when the Conversation for Withdrawal and Disengagement is missing:

- Sticking around too long in a situation that is not good for us and accepting something less than we could have
- Not seeing the patterns and therefore creating the same situation again
- Feeling chronically angry in the relationship if our boundaries are repeatedly ignored
- Feeling anger or fear if we are criticized constantly without acknowledgment of our strengths and contributions

Final Words

We will not want to work with everyone we meet in the business sphere, just as we will not want to be friends with everyone we meet in our personal lives. When I ask groups if they agree with the preceding statement, everyone in the audience immediately agrees. Then I ask my audience to turn it around: Do you expect everyone to want to work with you? Often it is not personal when someone else does not want to work with or become close friends with us.

Sometimes we need to admit to ourselves that we are in a toxic or one-sided relationship that is causing more problems than it is worth. In these cases it is best to end the connection so that we can invest our time in relationships that are meaningful and enjoyable. Walking away can be the best and most respectful choice if we do not want to invest the time and emotional energy into working through the issues, especially with those who are unwilling to share their issues or hear ours.

We do not owe people a long, drawn-out, detailed explanation about why we want to end the connection if the people we want to move away from have severely crossed our boundaries. We are not responsible for their growth, and they are not likely to hear us if we try to help them mature.

CHAPTER 14

Conversation for Change

If what you are doing is getting the results you want, keep doing it. If not, it is time to step up and make a change. Change is an individual choice. When we choose to change our behavior and beliefs, or the behavior of other people, then our conversations will have to change too. We have to bring others along to understand how we went from one way of thinking or operating to another way, and why they may want to as well. The way to do so is with a Conversation for Change. This is what Gandhi meant when he said, "Let us be the change we want to see in the world." If we do not have a conversation that helps others to understand the change in our thinking, we create a gap between ourselves and other people. We have to show others what we have changed so they can join in too.

Use this conversation when:

- A significant change is needed or has just occurred.
- A new leader joins the organization or team.
- A team member's performance is not meeting expectations.
- Your boundaries need to be changed or reinforced.
- You want open dialogue about current reality and the desired state.
- You are undertaking a new mission.

All about Change

According to Jack Welch, CEO of General Electric, "If you're not confused, you don't know what's going on." Change is everywhere, in every industry and business. It is hard to imagine an organization today that is not deep in the process of adapting to internal and external changes. Yet during the course of my working with an executive team, I have witnessed the president of an organization keep his head in the sand about the current reality and the direction in which the organization is headed. Fear causes some people to keep blinders on so that they do not see what is right in front of them. Leaders need to be aware of current reality and how it is impacting where their organization, customers, and employees are going. Given what is going on in the world today, when the Conversation for Change is not occurring within an organization, the end may be in sight for that organization. Asking the question, "What do we want to do to improve or grow?" and asking customers the same question will always generate possibilities. We want to grow and evolve; this requires change.

I have had the opportunity to work with many health-care, insurance, and pharmaceutical companies that have experienced huge changes in the past year. Yesterday I visited a pharmaceutical company that has created a café it refers to as the Brave Café, and next to it is the Brave Conference Area with a variety of different-sized meeting rooms that look and feel like private living rooms. The leadership at this company realized the importance of encouraging people to be brave in their communication with each other and with patients, doctors, and insurance companies. The leadership wanted this commitment to brave communication to be obvious and to stick around. Being brave enough to look at the current reality and build a vision to the desired future is vital to Conversations for Change.

Jack Taylor is the leader of the maintenance sales team for a software company. For 15 years he was part of a growing business that went from just a few employees to hundreds of employees, and from a million dollars in revenue to more than $100 million in revenue. Each year there were incremental changes in the organization, with evidence of 10+ percent growth in business. Also, each year he would discuss with his team members what priorities and actions would need to shift as a result of the goal to grow the business. Last year, a global giant purchased Jack's company, the company he helped build from the ground up. Now, most things about Jack's work are different.

Jack shared with me that the changes have been more challenging than he could have imagined. Learning all the new policies, procedures, and systems while continuing to sell to customers has been exciting and scary at the same time. The new organization has single contracts that gross the same revenue that his contracts collectively would produce in years past. Thus, the $200 contracts that Jack's team delivers are a hassle to the new organization and not worth its time. It does not make a difference to Jack what the dollar value of the contract is because he has been focused on helping and serving customers. He says, "I treat every customer pretty much the same. It is very different now in this large company. The mental, psychological leap from feeling like a person with a first and last name to now feeling like a number is so odd. I'm still dealing with this change months after it happened."

The change was tangible for him and his coworkers. The company had a new logo, new business cards, and new e-mail addresses. Everyone knew that a significant change had occurred. Jack has had to have many conversations with his management and peers about the response needed to succeed in this new environment. And as the leader of a team, he has had to share with his team members his own experiences so that they could stay connected, create a new plan for how best to approach their new reality, and produce results that meet the higher level of expectations placed on them.

This was not the case for Robin. She told me, "It seems like my boss expects me to be an analyst and a strategist. I just want her to tell me what to do so I can go do it." Robin had been in

181

her position for over 10 years when a new leader came into the organization. For the past year, this new leader has been suggesting that Robin needs to be "in front of what is happening, planning for upcoming change that may be occurring, building stronger partnerships and relationships in the organization, and being internal customer focused." At least that is how Robin heard the boss's request. Robin thinks all this is busy work that is pulling her away from what she is supposed to be focused on. I met with Robin's boss, Donna. She told me she was really struggling with Robin because she was not embracing all the duties of her position. Donna's view was that Robin was being resistant and stubborn, unwilling to do her new job. I asked Donna, "Have you ever said to Robin: 'The position you are in is a new one. It is not the job you had three years ago. The work has changed, and as a result, the responsibilities and expectations of your role are different'?"

Donna said that she'd had numerous conversations with Robin spelling out individual expectations, asking her to be more strategic in her work, and urging her to get out in front of planning for the new rules for this project. Donna admitted that she had never verbalized to Robin that the role was very different from the written job description that had been in place for many years before she arrived. Robin could not see a tangible logo showing that a profound shift had occurred and thus she was making the issue about Donna's leadership and communication style.

Donna and I role-played to help her create a Conversation for Change with Robin that sounded something like this:

> Robin, you have been a long-term employee here, and I value the experience you have with this organization. Thank you for the know-how and history you bring to our team.
>
> I can imagine how challenging the past year has been with the dramatic changes in our organization, the industry, and your leader. Robin, I need to be clear that the position you are in has evolved over the past year such that the expectations of the role are substantially

different. The position requires more than merely implementing plans created by me. I've outlined on paper the expectations I have for the role you are in. I'd like to discuss these expectations for the director role with you and then give you some time to think about this change. You can let me know later if this is a position you would want or if you want to consider other options.

A few days after this conversation, Robin said to me, "I am relieved. I am realizing that the issues were not personal between Donna and me, but rather the difference in my position was not clear to me. I had not seen the line drawn in the sand that this was a new job. The job changed, and I did not know it. The new job is not one I would want, and I can see that I would be happier if I moved into a role that is more focused on implementation and execution."

When change occurs within your organization, you need to verbalize it, because some people may not recognize that what they see as just the current reality is not a temporary thing. Rather, it's the new "normal." They may be thinking this is a blip on the radar, not an ongoing expectation. By creating a new logo, job description, vision statement, or other meaningful written description of the expected change, you help others to see the expectations that come from the change.

Embracing a Conversation for Change

When we initiate the change ourselves, we are often excited about the plan. When we see it as an exciting adventure that we signed up for, we probably feel hopeful. When someone else initiates the change and we experience it being thrust upon us, it is not uncommon to feel anger or fear. Having the emotional intelligence to deal with our own emotions first gives us the confidence and ability to navigate through the change.

According to Nigel Paine, a professor in the business school at Wharton, "You can change a professional business person's life by giving him or her a Kindle or iPad and an iPhone and teaching how to use them." Nigel makes a case for using technology to create a Conversation for Change with executives. By demonstrating how to use an application to solve a problem, you are engaging them in just such a conversation. We learned in grade school that show and tell is fun. It is also a compelling way to address needed change that may trigger fear or anger to jump over these emotions by tangibly showing the impact of the changed behavior.

I led a mentoring program for a group of high-potential future leaders. In the recent kickoff meeting, we asked the mentees what they want to focus on in their relationships with their mentors. This is what they said:

- "Get advice on how to grow the business"
- "Help me see next-step career options"
- "Determine how best to use my talents"
- "Learn about team building—how to lead other people to come together to make things happen"
- "Learn how to handle conflict and challenges"
- "Explore how U.S. and Chinese companies work best together"
- "Learn to delegate more effectively so I can lead bigger projects"
- "Model communication skills, and guide me to create new conversations"

These future leaders are eagerly asking for conversations focused on changing and growing. They are initiating the change they want to occur. They are feeling hopeful and excited to engage in conversations about these topics. Imagine if the same list was your own agenda in an organization and you were telling your team that this was now expected of them. Because someone else was initiating a change, the emotional tenor of the conversation might be different. If you were leading the Conversation for Change, in this case you would want to anticipate that the emotional reaction might be fear and anger. You would need to plan in time for team members to work through their own emotions.

If they are highly emotionally intelligent, the experience will look very different than if they are emotionally illiterate.

This ability to recognize the emotional impact of change is one that we can use in all parts of our lives. Our ability to change the conversation at home is the same as the ability to change conversations at work. Our ability to manage or lead a conversation does not change just because we've gotten on the phone with a work colleague or driven into the office. We use the same skills and know-how in the office that we use in conversations at home and in our social life.

Business is a conversation, and lately the predominant conversation in business is change. We do not have to be overwhelmed by that if we know how to be emotionally intelligent, flexible, and innovative. *Fast Company* is a high-circulation magazine that challenges and inspires conversations about the ways in which businesses, industries, and our lives are changing. In an article titled "It's a New Year. Can We Change the Conversation?" written by the founding editors of *Fast Company* on December 19, 2007, they say:

> Business is fundamentally a conversation. If we allow a focus on business gone wrong to crowd out any discussion of what might go right, if we allow the number crunchers to overwhelm the idea people, we make it harder to change the negative trends that we all find so, well, negative. Business conversation is the source of new ideas, new energy, and new directions. It shapes what we work on and how we work on it, day in and day out. What we talk about—with employees, with customers, and with colleagues—is a powerful force in determining what actually happens inside companies.

Sometimes the issue is that people are not letting go of their own resentment that the business, industry, or world has in fact changed and it is not going back to the way they liked it better before. Today is the day someone in the future is looking back at and calling it the good old days. How can you change that mindset for yourself?

Boundaries and Changing Patterns

Say you buy a new home in a new development, built on what was previously a large farm. Survey experts come with special equipment and put stakes in the ground at the four corners of each property. In such a situation, you could consider locating a plant, a large rock, or some other object next to the stake in the ground, so that if someone removes the stake, you will still know where your boundaries are. Boundaries can be acknowledged with flowering plants or lovely trees, not just iron stakes in the ground. Boundaries can be acknowledged in the workplace too. They often show up in times of change.

I am continually learning how and when to communicate my boundaries and stand up for my emotional lines in the sand. I've repeated this relationship dynamic many times with bosses, CEOs, colleagues, and mentors. By not being assertive about my emotional boundaries on some occasions in the past, I've acted powerless and deferred the agenda to their needs, tastes, and wants. If I do this too long, then I feel anger. This happens in any working relationship when I do not feel heard.

When we change roles in our work—for example, moving from being an individual contributor to being a manager or from being a manager to being a vice president—the boundaries change too. We need to be prepared for these exact types of changes, conscious of the shift that needs to change in the type of conversations we have.

I recently had a meeting with a colleague. We had a delightful conversation discussing work projects. For some reason, during the meeting he asked me about my divorce years ago, and he shared a bit about his own recent divorce. Everything felt good in the moment and I was comfortable to that point. Then he asked me, "Why did you get divorced?" I started to answer his question because we were enjoying the conversation, but I stopped as I got into the first paragraph. This was really none of his business and certainly not a place I needed to go for myself.

I was feeling my own boundary. I could feel this line in myself, and so I said, "To sum it up, we mutually came to the conclusion that it was best for us." And I put the conversation back on our business and moved the conversation along, aware of my own needs and boundaries. He wrote me a thank you note later, saying something like "Thank you for showing me a way to tell people why I got divorced without getting into the details. You changed my thinking on this."

The same thing happened when I watched two people in a meeting. Donna asked Mary, "Why would you leave a company like XYZ? They have been on the Best Places to Work list for the past several years." Mary smartly said, "I knew it was the best thing for me to do for myself." She did not have a need to romance the drama that existed around her leaving. Staying aware of boundaries serves everyone better than going down in the muck. We are a blessing to each other when we stay aware of our emotional wake.

Conversations Done Right

Here's how it sounds when a Conversation for Change goes well.

Kathy Oates

Kathy Oates, the vice president of leadership and organization development at GlaxoSmithKline, shared with me a recent example of how her organization engaged 1,000 leaders from the North American business in a Conversation for Change that is still having a positive impact. The leaders, managers, and employees met at a full-day meeting called "Join the Conversation." Starting with confirming their core values as an organization, the attendees sat together at round tables and engaged in dialogue focused on the following: "Where have we been successful in the past as individuals and as an organization? What needs to happen in the future to be successful? How do we want to model the change we want to see in our business? For example, if we say we want to be more customer focused, how are we modeling that, and what could we do more of?"

Kathy said, "This meeting sent a clear message that we need

to engage those that are closest to the business in helping design our future. Everyone in the meeting experienced being a part of changing the culture at GlaxoSmithKline in positive ways. The senior leaders regularly engage in listening conversations one-on-one at all levels of the organization as an example of living the organization's core values and embracing their commitment to engage everyone in creating meaningful change to grow the business." Kathy and her team clearly understood the importance of engaging people in a Conversation for Change.

Women in Leadership

The Women in Leadership group at a large pharmaceutical company decided to read Marshall Goldsmith's book *What Got You Here Won't Get You There*. The women asked me to facilitate a discussion of the book with a focus on the section "How We Can Change for the Better." To prepare for this discussion, each person was asked to identify a change she wanted to make and to come to the meeting ready to share. The discussion was lively and full of energy as executive-level women shared a specific change they wanted to make in their own leadership style.

Helen, a senior vice president who led a department of more than a hundred people, had courage when she stood up and said, "I've gotten feedback that some people experience me as being too arrogant and too often being late for meetings. I realize I must change the way I speak about my own abilities and how I show up at meetings since I cause others to feel like I do not value their time. I need to raise my awareness about when this is happening. Would you be willing to share with me when you see me do something that could appear arrogant?" Helen talked about specific behaviors she would need to change to be on time for all scheduled meetings. She identified whom she was going to ask to help her with this for the first month to hold her accountable so she would make the necessary changes.

The next time this group met, people acknowledged Helen for making these changes. She had been on time to every meeting and had been conscious of the way she might be perceived as speaking down to people. Her peers were supporting her and speaking about the changes in her behavior positively. This was just what she needed. If people do not know you are working on a change, they may not notice it as it is happening.

Kathy Koressel, the director of Talent Management, shared her experience:

> As a leader at a pharmaceutical company, I've had to create conversations with employees when serious change was needed in their performance for them to be able to stay in the organization. I have found it helpful to verbalize that the person I am speaking with has three choices:
>
> * You can stay and work with me while you change your performance.
> * You can stay and fight or resist this change and the need for improvement in your performance.
> * You can move on, creating your own change.
>
> I ask them to talk out with me the consequence of each choice as it relates to the changes needed on their part. Then I give them the choice and a few days to think about it. I express my support for whichever next step they decide even if it is disagreeing with my view of their performance. I'm not afraid of the conflict, and I make that clear in a nice way.

Phrases and Questions to Start a Conversation

Here are some ways to get your Conversation for Change started:

* "I have a dream that we could . . ."
* "A vision that really inspires me is . . ."
* "Google and Apple created positive change, and I think we can too if we . . ."

- "I am noticing what seems like shifting sands, and I want to check it out with you to see if you are experiencing these changes as well."
- "What would it look like if we were the best in . . ."
- "What would need to exist for us to embrace the new vision?"
- "Is there anything I need to forgive so I can be present in the moment now?"
- "Current reality is calling us to make some changes. Let's talk about what our experience of current reality is and how we can respond to it."
- "What have you noticed changing?"
- "Are there trends that are occurring around us that we have not yet discussed?"
- "If we got in front of the changes that we think are coming, what would it look like?"
- "How could we be proactive instead of reactive in this situation?"
- "What else do we think needs to change and why?"
- "What would we like the 'new normal' to be?"
- "How has another industry or business dealt with a current reality like the one we are experiencing now? What was the impact of the way they handled it?"
- "There is no such thing as 'We are all stable and will continue to be for years to come.' In light of this fact, I'd like to share some observations I have about trends that I think will lead to changes we need to be prepared for."
- "Can we learn from someone else's experience?"
- "Do you ever find yourself saying something like 'Once we get through this crazy period of change, then everything will return to normal'? I've realized that this belief is a problem because we will be faced with ongoing change. In fact, a trend I see that will bring about another round of change is . . ."
- "Our frenzied pace of change is the new 'normal.' Let's identify ways we can do a better job of helping others on

our team to understand why this is the truth so we can all become energized by the exciting possibilities offered by the changes."

Mistakes in Conversation

In a conflict between an existing culture and a desired change, the existing culture will come out the winner. There will be resistance to large-scale change, and it may not be logical to you. If you don't think there is any resistance, then you have your head in the sand. Remaining unaware of resistance is a common mistake people make during times of change. Be prepared to hear some illogical thinking. Listen, mull over what you hear, and then reply. If you want change to occur, you'll need to look at how people are being rewarded. If the rewards remain the same old way they were, the change will not occur.

Ideally you will involve the people who will be making the change in defining what will be changing. If you are not able to involve them in the "what" part of the decision, then include them in the "how" part of the decision to implement discussions and decisions.

Use the language that the people you are asking to change use. How do they speak to each other? Talk that way when explaining the change. Years ago a client hired me to lead a management workshop for a week for the managers who needed to develop new leadership skills. The senior executive who hired me asked, "Shawn, do you own a pair of jeans and cowboy boots? Your answer does not matter; the fact is you'll need them when you deliver this training if you want the managers to hear you." I bought a pair of jeans and cowboy boots to deliver that meeting because I was asking them to make a change in their skill level and they needed to hear my message if they wanted to be successful. I used their lingo and dressed in their style so that my words and clothes would not distract from my message. I made it an adventure for myself and shared that spirit with them. When I told them I'd changed into jeans and boots to deliver this message, they loved it.

Tia Finn, a manager from Pearson Digital, shares this example:

> Four years ago our company was in the midst of a massive internal merger. Change was happening in so many areas and at such a rapid pace that the tensions and stresses were tangible. When the world you had gotten comfortable in suddenly turns upside down, there is a strong feeling of fear. And when you combine stress, fear, and the unknown, it is easy for panic to set in, derailing all forward progress. At our quarterly managers meeting, our senior leader asked the group, "How do we get our folks more comfortable with change?"
>
> I had been reading a lot about change management, change motivation, and change leadership during those difficult days. What I began to realize is the way to get folks comfortable with change, is to stop talking about "change." Our mistake was over focusing on the word "change" and not on what we wanted to create. Change happens everyday everywhere. We want to be strategic, and we must be agile in our ability to morph to the needs of the market. Inherent in this process is continuous change. But the word itself can carry so much anxiety that it becomes a catalyst for dysfunction. Instead I suggested we focus on changing the words we were using in the conversation. So now we talk about strategic agility, and our ability to flex our approach, skills, and communications to fit the needs of our internal and external customers each day. We've taken the word "change" out of our business vocabulary and in doing so removed much of the fear and anxiety attached to the word. Instead you hear people talking about innovation and creative ideation and flexing department structures and development processes to meet customer and business needs. We are still changing every day, but it feels exciting now!

When There's No Conversation

The following problems can result when the Conversation for Change is missing:

- We do not innovate or create new products and services.
- Without meaningful conversation about what needs to change in our company in order to thrive in today's world, our competition may make huge leaps beyond us with their offerings.
- Without meaningful conversation about what needs to change in our lives for us to be able to live our best life, we often do not take time to take care of our own health or progress in our careers.
- We may ignore the impact that a newly announced, significant change will have on our department or team.
- We may not recognize that when a new leader joins the organization or team, it will impact relationships.
- Ignoring the performance of a team member who is not meeting expectations and who needs to change will cause more trouble for the whole team, and we may not admit that to ourselves.

Final Words

Change is everywhere. Change can trigger deep emotional reactions in ourselves and others. Having the emotional intelligence to identify and regulate our own emotions gives us the confidence and ability to navigate through changes. Fear and anger will occur for each of us in the face of unexpected change that we did not want to occur. This type of change that we did not initiate for ourselves often requires us to let go of resentment and to forgive someone or something. This is an emotional issue, and a Conversation for Change demands understanding of how emotions work.

When you are initiating a change that will impact other people, expect that they will have to work through their own emotions. Give them time to do this and perhaps help to process them through their emotions by asking questions in a supportive manner. Use the language that the people who are asking for the change use in their daily conversations with each other. Make the change visible in some form so it is not just words and concepts.

Conversation for Appreciation

A little appreciation goes a long way. (With that in mind, allow me to take a moment to thank you for sticking with me through these chapters.) Conversations for Appreciation are uplifting deposits into the emotional bank account between people. You have likely created many of these in the past. They specifically acknowledge the contributions others have made. Hopefully you have not waited until now to create a Conversation for Appreciation. These conversations can be used anytime you sincerely want to express gratitude. They can be built into some of the previous conversations that may have several meetings to get to resolution.

Use this conversation when:

- You are developing new skills in yourself or others.
- You are grateful for the progress that has been made.
- You want to say thank you in a meaningful way.
- You want to customize your appreciation to the style of the person you are thanking.
- You want a stronger relationship that generates endorsement from another person or a group.
- You are endorsing others.

All about Appreciation

Being able to create a meaningful conversation that acknowledges and triggers feelings of appreciation is vital to building momentum in relationships. Think of the last time you felt really appreciated. What happened to cause you to feel this? I am going to guess that someone showed appreciation to you in the language that works best for you; he or she sincerely spoke to your values and communication style. When this happens, we feel joyful. Understanding communication styles and values enables us to see the strengths that each individual brings to the team or conversation.

Saying "thank you" triggers positive feelings in both the speaker and the listener. Many executives I work with have a file folder where they keep the thank you notes they have received. I have the thank you note my first boss wrote me after I completed a huge project for him more than 20 years ago. Sara, the president of a professional services company, has a shelf behind her desk where she keeps the thank you notes that people wrote in the past few months. It reminds her that her clients appreciate the work she does for them. She feels hope and love when she looks at this shelf.

Different Ways to Show Appreciation

There are four basic ways of showing appreciation at work:

1. *Affirmation.* Conversation pointing out what someone does well, saying "thank you," or encouraging you. Pointing out to individuals their strengths and the ways they add value to the team can produce amazing connections.
2. *Quality time.* Doing something together or just really listening and sharing with each other. At work it may look like taking time to answer questions or coaching and training someone for the next level of growth. Or it could be "couch time." Have you noticed when you sit on a couch with someone and there is no TV

or other distractions, you really focus on the conversation together?

3. *Gifts.* Giving an item or an experience that the other person wants—for example, when you get a Mont Blanc pen from a boss who thanks you for writing her thank you notes for her.

4. *Acts of service.* Doing something to help the other person. It might be keeping your word and doing what you say you will or sharing something you think will benefit the other person. It could also be something like completing a project on time, on budget, and with no surprises.

Acts of service are the way I most prefer to be shown that I'm appreciated, followed by affirmation in conversation. One of the consultants on my team who I discussed this with has the same feeling. Knowing this enables us to think of ways to show appreciation in the language of the other person. Thinking about my colleague's preferred appreciation language enables me to connect in a more meaningful way.

Deb works with me in my office. Prior to joining my company, she worked for a doctor who did not take the time to show appreciation. As a result, she felt she wasn't receiving feedback and she did not know where she stood in her work. This caused her to look for a new position. After we had worked together for four months, Deb shared with me that acts of service is her top way of receiving appreciation. She pointed out that my providing her a laptop computer to work with from her home, creating custom office space that fits her needs, and including her in decisions that impact her work made her feel appreciated. She said that when she feels appreciated, she wants to grow in her work and feels committed to her role. One thank you begets another.

Employees need regular tokens of appreciation for the work they are doing. Saying "Thank you for . . ." and explaining *in detail* what they did that helped you or the team is meaningful. However, if that is the only way you express appreciation, you may miss the mark. Vary the forms of gratitude you bestow on your coworkers. Once, I baked homemade cookies and hand-delivered them to each member on my team with a special thank you to each person for working long hours and focusing on a client project. Giving a gift certificate for a cup of coffee (or something else a person would enjoy) is a nice way to thank someone for something small. Giving a gift certificate to an office supply store if an employee needs decor or supplies for work shows a commitment to an employee and triggers feelings of loyalty.

Giving Experiences

Giving experiences as gifts can be loads of fun. Taking colleagues you appreciate to a new restaurant, meeting venue, or coffee shop can create a memorable experience. An executive in a marketing company, Jane, decided to thank her top customers by taking them all to the Four Seasons for high tea. This produced many memorable connections, which were gifts too.

When Elizabeth Jeffries, a longtime mentor and colleague on my team, visited us in our Philadelphia office it was close to her birthday, and I wanted to create a special celebration for her. I remembered that her favorite kind of cuisine was Southern Italian, and so I made arrangements for us to have dinner at this fabulous restaurant in Philadelphia that specialized in authentic Southern Italian cooking. The food was amazing, and the accordion player sang as if we were all on a gondola together. Giving this experience as a birthday gift meant more to her than another pair of earrings or some other item would have. Such experiences create memories that will be there whenever either of us needs to remember what our cherished relationship is about.

Saying Thank You

You may recall Tim, one of my coaching clients, who had been struggling with being perceived as overly judgmental of others. His relationships with his peers were suffering as a result. As part of our work together, I asked Tim to see if he experienced what

I do when I write a heartfelt thank you note to someone—I feel great! I also shared with him that if I look for things to appreciate, I can find many opportunities to thank someone. I asked Tim to send a thank you note each day of the week to see what would happen. He wrote his assistant, telling her how much he valued the fact that she was willing to fill in his blind spots. Another day he wrote to one of his clients, thanking her for being an ongoing supporter of their work. He became inspired. He decided to send a card to a colleague he'd met at a professional association. He told the colleague how much he appreciated her contribution to the association they participate in. When the week was over, he did not want to stop sending an inspired card each day because it made him feel great too. And something else began to happen. A week later he started getting a call each day from the person he'd sent the card to the prior week. He got to talk with someone who appreciated his gesture. Tim began to see that Conversations for Appreciation can change relationships dramatically. He is on the lookout for things to appreciate, and now many are showing up.

Quick Notes

Sometimes the best way to show appreciation for a colleague or a client is through a quick note, rather than a full conversation. The following are examples of how you can express your appreciation to someone in writing.

> "Thank you, Kemba, for double-checking all my numbers in the report for the new client. Your effort made a difference in our ability to get that report out quickly."

> "I appreciate that you asked me those questions in the meeting last week, Juan. They kept me on track, got me focused, and helped me to understand where you are in your own thinking at this time. Keep the questions coming."

> "Joyce, I'd like to invite you to lunch or dinner to thank you for all the effort you put into planning for the conference. You made

the conference seem like it was a breeze by creating an agenda that flowed easily, working with the conference center to nail down the contract details, and ensuring that all the participants had the information they needed prior to the event."

"Janice, you have done a great job of editing my work. Thank you so much for your effort and wonderful suggestions! I especially appreciate how easy you are to work with and how clear your recommendations are."

When you do not know someone well enough yet to appreciate something specific about them, perhaps say something like "I am looking forward to getting to know you" or "I've heard good things about you and anticipate you'll add a lot of value to our department."

And when someone is acknowledging you, accept the compliment rather than say, "You shouldn't have" or "I don't deserve this." Listen and take it in when people acknowledge you. Their endorsement points to something you've done that is worth repeating and provides clues about who they are and what they appreciate too.

Conversations Done Right

Here are some examples of how a Conversation for Appreciation sounds when it goes well.

Jane

When Jane, the leader of a project management team at an insurance company, realized her team had completed its mission, she invited all the team members and many of the senior managers to a company-sponsored celebration luncheon. She gave all the people attending the lunch their own stack of cards with everyone's name on them except their own name. Jane asked each person to write what he or she appreciated about the individuals whose names were on the cards. Then, at the lunch meeting, Jane said something specific about the contribution that each team member made. She also gave members of the team the opportunity to give one another positive feedback about the contributions they received from working together. Finally, they passed out their cards to one another—a bit like Valentine's Day—and each person left the luncheon with a trove of special acknowledgment cards. Jane created a healthy ending in this Conversation for Appreciation, realizing that some of the people on this team she would likely work with again on other projects and others she may never see again. Jane then had a private conversation with herself about what she wanted to create next in her career as a result of completing this huge project successfully.

Tom

Tom was disappointed when his assistant, Kindra, had to move to another state due to her husband's job relocation. He had appreciated the way they worked so well together. He knew that Kindra would likely have a challenge finding a new position in a state where she knew no one. Tom also believed that Kindra would fit in very well in a company in the state she was about to move to. So he called the company to ask if it had any openings. He spoke with the managers and informed them that Kindra was moving to their area. He paved the way for her to be able to work at an organization he knew she would really enjoy. Tom expressed his appreciation by creating new opportunities for Kindra.

When Kindra started her new position, she sent Tom a heartfelt thank you letter highlighting all the things she appreciated about him as a manager. Kindra also recommended Tom's organization to a company that needed his services. Endorsement begets endorsement.

Michael

Michael, a senior leader of a well-respected university, worked with a coach for six months. He liked the coach enough to write an endorsement on her LinkedIn page. This endorsement meant a great deal to her, and as a result, the coach wanted to do more helpful things to support Michael in his role.

The law of reciprocity shows up when we give endorsements to others, as they are more likely to return the favor the next time the opportunity arises to do so. Consultants, independent contractors, and job seekers are not the only ones who appreciate a public endorsement of their abilities and contributions on LinkedIn. We all do.

Phrases and Questions to Start a Conversation

Here are some ways to get your Conversation for Appreciation started:

- "Thank you for . . ."
- "The reason I really appreciate what you did is . . ."
- "I wanted to point out several things I've noticed that you have done very well recently . . ."
- "Jodi told me you really excel at . . ."
- "Susan, while Hiromi is standing here with us, I wanted to share with you some of the things that he has done recently to help our department. He has been a star because he . . ."
- "Congratulations on the successful completion of the XYZ project. Thank you for putting in so much time to ensure that all the details were handled."
- "What a great event you pulled off. I really enjoyed the . . ."
- "I can see you are going to be just what we need in this organization. I'm glad you are joining us."
- "That was the best meeting we've had. Thank you for doing such a good job facilitating our team meeting. You got everyone participating by asking such great questions, Meeta."
- "Thank you for doing your best on this webinar. I really liked the way you . . ."
- "I am writing you this thank you note because I wanted you to know how much it meant to us that you . . ."

- "Because appreciation is so personal and I want to do something nice to acknowledge you, I'd like to know what your favorite restaurant is so I can treat you to lunch to thank you for . . ."

Mistakes in Conversation

When you are not specific about what you are appreciative of, your expression of thanks will ring hollow and not have the desired impact. The gratitude may be well intentioned, but a lack of specifics reflects form, not substance. What can also be a mistake, especially to the person to whom the appreciation is due, is thanking everyone on the team for what was really the effort of one person. This may trigger feelings of anger for the person deserving the gratitude and likely will cause embarrassment for the other team members and a realization that no one cared enough to "get the story straight." On the flip side, thanking one person for the efforts of a team is also bound to raise the frustration level and ire of those not being recognized and can have far-reaching negative consequences for the next project. After all, why bother if someone else will get the credit anyway?

And don't talk yourself out of expressing appreciation because you are afraid that if you thank someone, the person will expect a raise or a promotion. Recall a boss who rarely said thank you or acknowledged your contribution to the team. How often did you go the extra mile for him or her? In essence, it is a mistake *not* to engage in Conversations for Appreciation often. Keep in mind that it takes five positive interactions to dilute one negative one, so better to build your reserves!

When There's No Conversation

The following problems can result when the Conversation for Appreciation is missing:

- Employees are not likely to go the extra mile and may feel unwanted.

203

- Conflicts emerge more frequently in situations when there is no appreciation.
- Tight, cold, critical cultures are created when accomplishments are not acknowledged and grateful "thank yous" are not expressed.

Final Words

A sincere thank you with a specific example of what the other person did to contribute is like making a deposit in an emotional bank account. Being able to create a meaningful conversation that acknowledges and triggers feelings of appreciation is vital to building momentum in relationships. Expressing gratitude triggers positive feelings in both the speaker and the listener.

One thing that we all have in common is that we like to be endorsed. We love to be acknowledged. Our employees may need more acknowledgments from us than we are accustomed to giving. For a few weeks make a point to individually verbalize the strengths and contributions of each person on your team. As you endorse the members individually for their unique strengths and contributions, you will notice the relationship's emotional bank account grow. Vary the forms of gratitude you use; consider affirmation, gifts, acts of service, and quality time together focused on helping them with their goals or answering questions that help them grow. Giving experiences as gifts can be loads of fun and will create lasting memories.

When someone is acknowledging you, accept the compliment. Marinate in the positive feeling, and let yourself experience it. Don't say, "You shouldn't have" or "I don't deserve this," because it diminishes the gift.

Destructive conflicts emerge more frequently in situations when there is no appreciation and acknowledgment of people's strengths and contributions. The law of reciprocity shows up when we give endorsements to others, as they are more likely to return the favor the next time an opportunity arises to do so.

Conversation for Moving On

Moving to a new office space, retiring from a company, and taking a position with another company are examples of times when we create Conversations for Moving On. Good–bye parties or lunches are a nice way to acknowledge when someone is withdrawing in a healthy way. We let go and move on, perhaps remembering one another with a friendly holiday or birthday card each year.

Use this conversation when:

- Someone is moving, retiring, or leaving the team, and you want to share how he or she contributed.
- A project is ending.
- You do not want to burn a bridge, and you would like the relationship to continue even though you will not be seeing each other regularly any more.
- You want to summarize what was done or acknowledge what was accomplished.
- It's time to let go of the current structure for how you connect.
- You want to create healthy endings.
- You are moving on.

All about Moving On

Most of us have met hundreds or perhaps thousands of other people in our lifetime. We do not typically maintain a close relationship with every person we meet. Classmates, coworkers, and former friends are among the many people who have entered our lives only to leave later on. One day we may reconnect, but for now we have closure with no expectation of communicating again soon.

We also need to individually let go and close chapters in our lives. Even when there are not natural end points, such as the end of a semester or a change in careers, there are times when we need to move on. A Conversation for Moving On helps put the punctuation in place that emotionally closes the connection for now. Once we have done this, then we can be prepared to start another Conversation for Creating New Possibilities.

When my husband left Johnson & Johnson after 24 years of employment there, his boss had a good-bye party for him at a lovely restaurant. People spoke publicly and privately about the impact of his contribution to the team. They gave him gifts that demonstrated how much they appreciated working with him. This created a special memory for him.

Jean, Isabel, and Alano had been in a fast-paced MBA program together for the past two years. They had worked on so many projects with one another, they could not believe that now as they were graduating, they would not be seeing each other often. Two days after graduation, they got together to have a final lunch before they moved on to their new roles in different cities. At this lunch their conversation was about appreciating the time they had together and moving on.

Moving On with a Memorable Experience

A client, Deborah Herting, PMP, from Aetna shared her own personal experience of a meaningful closing conversation:

One project I worked on had two false starts and three previous project managers. It was a highly visible, complex strategic project. When I was assigned to the project, morale was low, with some key people wanting to transition off the project. An extremely knowledgeable Lead Business Analyst did leave the department. This left the team scrambling to gather requirements. Team members wanted to know how we would know what questions to ask to obtain mission-critical information. How would we know that all stones were being unturned so that a comprehensive deliverable could be achieved?

Fortunately, throughout a year-and-a-half period, a team was built where members took ownership, empowered themselves, cared for each other, and shared information willingly. We openly communicated and were proactive in addressing risks and issues.

At the end of the project, company management sent congratulatory e-mails. However, for the team leads who had worked together cohesively and through much adversity, those notes were not enough. We had truly bonded as a team.

Despite working in a virtual environment, with over two hundred team members dispersed in many different locations, we planned a closing dinner. At our own expense, we planned a night out together. Choosing a restaurant at a convenient location, as a project management team, we enjoyed an evening together where we shared stories, laughed, and cried about our experiences. It was refreshing!

Three years later, many of the leads on this team maintain a close relationship. We acknowledge each other on holidays despite significant cultural diversities. We catch up on personal news related to our families. We are there for each other for work-related questions, and we often check in with each other.

When we find ourselves on conference calls together for new projects, we always say it's good to hear your voice. That usually follows with an Instant Message emoticon of a smiley face. This team closed our project by celebrating our success. By doing so, it helped each team member transition to our next assignment with a significant success to feel proud of. It also meant the beginning of authentic work relationships built from the challenges that come with a complex project assignment, yet facilitated by open communication and trust.

Conversations Done Right

Here are some examples of what it sounds like when a Conversation for Moving On goes well.

Faith

Faith managed a large technical department that required new employees to pass a certification exam after completing a two-month training program. In the hiring process for new employees, the management team did its best to ensure it was hiring someone who would be able to stick with the intense training and pass the exam.

Faith optimistically hired a young man named Mike. At the time that Mike was hired, at least 40 other people had previously been through the training and passed the exam successfully. Mike was just out of college and a bit younger than the average person who was hired. Maybe that had something to do with why he was often late for the 8 a.m. training class. He did well in the afternoon classes and participated in group discussions. It appeared that he stayed up late at night and was very tired during the mornings, and as a result, he seemed to miss a few hours of material each morning. The class instructors explained to Mike several times that it was important for him to attend the whole class and that it would be hard for him to pass the exam if he missed the mornings. Because the instructors kept Faith informed along the way, it did not come as a surprise to her when she learned that Mike failed the final certification exam and thus his employment would be terminated. This is how Faith handled the conversation with Mike.

Faith: *Mike, you have many talents that we've seen during the two months you have been here. We hired you because we liked your ability* *to problem-solve, to think through complex issues, and your ability to discuss solutions to issues. Unfortunately, you did not pass the certification exam. That means we are not able to continue your employment. (Long pause.)*

Mike: *Is there any way I can retake the test? I really want this job. I thought I would sail through the exam like I did in college.*

Faith: *Mike, we are not able to continue your employment. Our policy is clear, and we have quizzes along the way in the class so you are able to gauge your own progress and understanding of the material. This one exam is not the story of your professional life. Something about this situation did not work for you at this time. Figure out what that is so that you can meet the expectations of the work you want to do. I'd like to hear from you in a few months to know what you are doing. The door is open for us to talk again if you would like to reach out to me.*

Mike: *Thank you, Faith. I am really disappointed in myself. I will follow up with you and let you know what I decide to do next, and I will call you a year from today so we can talk about what is happening then.*

In a positive postscript to this story, Mike and Faith did keep in touch beyond Mike's brief employment at her company. Mike ended up finding a technical job that started at 11 a.m., and he seems to be happy working that shift.

Donna and Robin

Do you recall Robin and Donna from Chapter 14 on Conversations for Change? Robin's role changed dramatically over a two-year period. Her new leader, Donna, needed to create a conversation that underscored the fact that Robin's position was no longer the same job she had done for 10 years. Her new role was that of a long-term planner, where she was expected to be more strategic and aware of upcoming trends. After absorbing this reality and the significance of the changes, Robin decided that the position was no longer a good fit for what she liked to do. Her values were no longer being rewarded by the accountabilities expected from the role. Robin decided to play to her own strengths as an implementer and someone who could execute well once a strategy was formulated. Robin admitted to herself that she wanted to change. But she did not want to burn a bridge with Donna. Robin wanted Donna's support in finding a new role that would better suit her natural talents.

Robin scheduled an appointment with Donna and began the conversation by saying: "The conversation we had about how dramatically the expectations of my position have changed over the past year was helpful. I've admitted to myself that I am in a different position even though the title stayed the same. Perhaps that is what you were trying to get me to see subtly over the past year or so, but I did not really see it until you drew a line in the sand when we spoke last week. Well, I've given it a great deal of thought, and I realize that my strengths are more aligned with implementing and executing a strategy rather than formulating the strategy. As a result, I'd like to explore opportunities within our company for me to move into a role that better uses my abilities. I'd like to continue to do the work in my role until I find another position that would better play to my strengths and support the business."

As a result of this candid conversation, Robin and Donna were able to close a chapter in their relationship with each other on a healthy note. Robin had been thinking and speaking about Donna as if she were a terrible manager, someone who was just making busy work for her. Donna thought that Robin was being resistant to her leadership style. Donna had not realized that because she had not clearly outlined to Robin the changes in Robin's role, Robin did not recognize that her job was fundamentally different. Now they could close the mistaken view that they each had of the other. This shifted their relationship profoundly.

Dan

In another real-life example of a Conversation for Moving On, Dan led a large, global, cross-functional project team that was pulled together for a year to work on rebranding for his company's core products. The company wanted customers to realize that all the products were part of the core company brand. This team was charged with shifting customers' views to see these products in new ways as part of a unified offering. First, the company had to discontinue the way it was speaking about some products internally and begin to use new language. Once that happened within the company, then the new language could be introduced to customers. As part of the rebranding process, the company decided to change some of the product names. As a tangible close to the old product names, the team invited employees and customers to trade in their sweatshirts and T-shirts that had the former product names on them for new ones with the new product names. Activities like this made a tangible difference that enabled customers to begin to think and speak differently. Formally ending the use of the old product names created a sense of moving on and starting fresh.

With some of the other globally known products, the company wanted to keep the recognized product names. This required more intention around having customers close their old notions about how the products worked and instead see the new features and services that aligned to all the other products as the most important aspects to discuss. The team held customer meetings to demonstrate why speaking in new ways about the products benefited everyone.

Phrases and Questions to Start a Conversation

Here are some ways to get your Conversation for Moving On started:

- "I wanted to take a few minutes to acknowledge our work together on the XYZ team as we prepare to move on."
- "You made an impact on this project by doing . . ."
- "Thank you for all the effort you put into . . . I wish you all success in future projects."
- "You are my new role model for integrity, and I wanted to share with you an example of something you did that causes me to say this . . . may I connect with you again when I am on another project and need your role modeling?"

- "The next time I need help with . . . , I'd like to call you to see if you are available."
- "Perhaps you'd like me to introduce you to Donna, who is also passionate about . . . The two of you would enjoy knowing each other now that you have more free time on your hands."

Mistakes in Conversation

The biggest mistake people make in this conversation is not having the conversation at all or passing over it nonchalantly with little thought. There are some things to keep in mind when having Conversations for Moving On. Start with a Conversation for Appreciation when you are able to be sincere. Take the time to acknowledge what you are moving on to, and trade contact information so you can stay connected. This is where LinkedIn can be valuable, because if you link up with others, you will have their contact information as they move around from company to company or location. The Conversation for Moving On is a way to show who we are as mature, respectful professionals. It seals the memory of working together to a positive story about the impact and value of your joint experience. If a relationship needs a story that reframes what was learned from a challenging time together, this is an opportunity to create that new story.

When There's No Conversation

The following problems can result when the Conversation for Moving On is missing:

- We lose contact with someone we enjoyed knowing or working with.
- We burn a bridge unknowingly.
- We give the impression that we did not appreciate the support or help that was offered before we moved on.

- We may not feel as if things ended on a good note and resist reconnecting if we hear of a job lead that could be of interest to the other person.

Final Words

When a project ends or we leave for another job and no acknowledgment of others occurs, we just drift off and miss an opportunity to have a meaningful conversation. This conversation could seal the memory of working together to a positive story about the impact and value of our joint experiences. A Conversation for Moving On helps put the punctuation in place that emotionally closes a connection for now. Once we have done this, then we can be prepared to start a new Conversation for Creating New Possibilities.

Putting It All Together: The Conversation Map

Now that we have discussed the 12 types of conversations, let's explore how they can fit together as a road map for you to choose which type of conversation you want to engage in based on what is happening in your relationship.

Conversations can be a meaningful gift. When we are intentional in our ability to connect with others and create conversations, we provide meaning. Our ability to help people get through a stuck spot, or inspire them to see a new possible vision for their career, or even just listen when they need to think out their own next actions—each of these can be a gift to others. Think of a few people you really appreciate. Most likely what you will realize is that their conversation ability contributes something positive to your work and life. They talk with you in a way that makes you feel as if they get what you are saying. They take action based on your conversations. This builds meaningful, long-term relationships. It is not just one conversation, but rather many built over time, that grows an emotional bank account that is a huge gift.

I hope that you enjoyed reading this book and that you are able to begin to use it immediately to change your conversation. I hope you use it to create more meaning in your work by being

When the Conversation Changes Journey Map

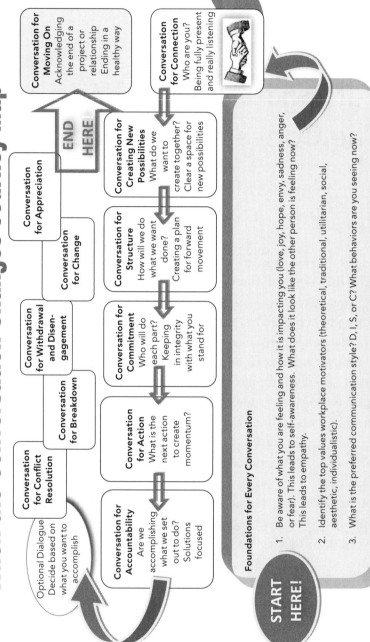

Conversation for Moving On
Acknowledging the end of a project or relationship Ending in a healthy way

Conversation for Connection
Who are you? Being fully present and really listening

END HERE

Conversation for Appreciation

Conversation for Creating New Possibilities
What do we want to create together? Clear a space for new possibilities

Conversation for Withdrawal and Disengagement

Conversation for Change

Conversation for Structure
How will we do what we want done? Creating a plan for forward movement

Conversation for Breakdown

Conversation for Conflict Resolution

Conversation for Commitment
Who will do each part? Keeping in integrity with what you stand for

Conversation for Action
What is the next action to create momentum?

Optional Dialogue
Decide based on what you want to accomplish

Conversation for Accountability
Are we accomplishing what we set out to do? Solutions focused

Foundations for Every Conversation

1. Be aware of what you are feeling and how it is impacting you (love, joy, hope, envy, sadness, anger, or fear). This leads to self-awareness. What does it look like the other person is feeling now? This leads to empathy.

2. Identify the top values workplace motivators (theoretical, traditional, utilitarian, social, aesthetic, individualistic).

3. What is the preferred communication style? D, I, S, or C? What behaviors are you seeing now?

START HERE!

intentional in the conversations you initiate, rather than just passively participating in them. In order to bring the message of this book alive, you will need to practice what you learned. Over the next 30 to 60 days, each day think about which conversation types would be best for what you want to accomplish.

In Part I of this book, we discussed how the state of our emotions in the moment will have a significant impact on our frame of mind, our ability to engage, and our openness to new possibilities. Our current emotion will color our ability to see options in conversations that could be created next. When we are full of hope, we experience our options very differently than when we are worried and fearful.

When we speak to topics that align with the other person's top values, we are more likely to engage in conversations that would be meaningful to the other person. How we approach and behave in a conversation will be influenced by our own preferred communication style. When we adapt our style to the other person's communication needs, we are more likely to create a conversation that person can easily hear. *Emotional intelligence, workplace motivators,* and *preferred communication styles* form the foundation for all conversations we engage in. The more you familiarize yourself with yours, the easier you'll be able to understand other people's and achieve meaningful conversations.

In Part II of this book, you learned about the 12 different types of conversations and how to get the most out of them. You are now able to confidently use each conversation deliberately. Conversations for Connection will enable you to begin or develop relationships. Being clear in your goals and engaging in a Conversation for Creating New Possibilities will lead you to know what types of conversation you want to create in order to bring your goals alive. Then you can select the next conversation you need to have based on what shows up. What do you want to create?

Use the When the Conversation Changes Journey Map above as a guide to help you decide which type of conversation needs to be created next based on your goals. You can also use the chart that follows to understand how the communication styles will impact each of the 12 types of conversations.

Conversation	Communication style that naturally excels at this conversation	Style that most needs to develop ability in this type of conversation
Conversation for Connection	I: will reach out to meet new people	C: needs to learn the importance of this type of conversation and engagement
Conversation for Creating New Possibilities	D: will want to initiate new activities I: will want to verbalize lots of ideas in meetings C: will explore and research possibilities on his or her own	S: would prefer to continue doing things the way he or she has been doing them
Conversation for Structure	S: will want to discuss the process, the step-by-step sequence, and the pace	D and I: may not want to focus on these details because they want to jump in now to begin action
Conversation for Commitment	D: will be quick to agree but not necessarily stick with it for the long haul S: will stick with commitments the longest but may take the longest to come to agreement to begin	I: may agree but not follow through
Conversation for Action	D: will jump in immediately and be ready to go I: will jump in with excitement and enthusiasm	S: may struggle to initially get going, but once S gets going, he or she will continue the action C: wants to have explored all options before taking action
Conversation for Accountability	D: will hold others accountable directly C: will e-mail a request for a status update	S: may not be willing to directly hold others accountable and may do it for self instead

Conversation	Communication style that naturally excels at this conversation	Style that most needs to develop ability in this type of conversation
Conversation for Conflict Resolution	D: will put the interpersonal conflict out in the open but may jump to the first resolution option that appears I: will want to resolve the conflict once it is clear and will want to explore options	S: will not want to deal with open conflict; S may show passive-aggressive tendencies C: will not likely point out that there is an interpersonal conflict
Conversation for Breakdown	D: will verbalize that this is not working C: will work hard to find another way before verbalizing the breakdown	I: may be so busy that he or she has not noticed yet that a breakdown has occurred
Conversation for Withdrawal and Disengagement	D: willing to move on quickly	S & C: have a harder time letting go
Conversation for Change	I & D: enjoy variety and big-picture changes; may like change for the sake of change	C & S: will want to slow changes down and consider all options first
Conversation for Appreciation	I: natural at affirming others	C: may not realize why this conversation is needed; may be more focused on criticism
Conversation for Moving On	D: may already be on to the next thing I: will enjoy acknowledging others' contributions	S: will not want change to occur C: may gloss over the need for this conversation

How Other People Have Put It All Together

I had the opportunity to speak with a variety of people from different-sized organizations who wanted to influence the performance management process in their organizations. To give you an example of how others tied all the lessons of this book together, I'll share what some of those people have done.

Imagine these different scenarios, which required using a variety of the conversations to reach the desired results.

In an organization that did not meet its revenue goals, is it reasonable to say that the majority of the sales organization met or exceeded expectations on their performance reviews? Most people would say no. Yet that is what happened in one particular consumer packaged goods company. The sales leaders, Jennifer and Sam, initially rated all the sales team members with "meets expectations," "exceeds expectations," or "outstanding" ratings. The vice president of human resources, Dave, and the CEO, John, realized they needed to create a Conversation for Conflict Resolution to push back on the sales leaders, saying they would not accept these performance ratings given that the goals were not met.

How does this happen that leaders think performance exceeds expectations when the results are clearly below the agreed-upon expectations? When this occurs, it is likely the managers were not having meaningful, developmental conversations with their employees periodically throughout the year. They were not using the Conversation for Accountability when they needed to do so. Thus, when it came time to evaluate performance, these managers were not willing to surprise a sales representative with a "needs improvement" rating.

This is why companies created forced performance-ranking bell curves in the first place, because senior managers did not trust that the necessary conversations were occurring when they needed to. Are you familiar with the forced performance-ranking policies in corporations? These policies give managers a mandate that 70 percent of the staff must be rated "meets expectations" and 10 percent must be rated "needs improvement." Conversations for Accountability need to start at the top so that we can avoid these forced bell curves to be implemented as a Band-Aid.

I've spoken with many managers who do not think this policy is fair or reasonable, especially when they have small teams and they do not think anyone should be rated "needs improvement." They are living with deep internal conflict. How these managers have handled their Conversation for Conflict Resolution around this issue has varied. For some, this is a clear case in which a Conversation for Change needs to be created with the right stakeholders. Being aware of the preferred communication styles, motivators, and current emotions of each of the stakeholders will have an impact on the success of the conversations.

Senior management wants line managers to do their job and manage employees. And managers want to be able to decide with their direct report employee how that employee should be rated. Many organizations need to navigate this Conversation for Change in the way reviews and feedback are delivered. Which type of conversation would you begin with if this were an issue you wanted to influence in your organization?

Jennifer and Sam, the sales leaders from the consumer packaged goods company, decided they needed to start with a Conversation for Connection with Dave, the vice president of human resources. They wanted to understand Dave's view of the performance management system. They scheduled a meeting with Dave. Before the meeting, Jennifer and Sam identified that Dave's preferred communication style is a High Influencer with a Steady backup. Dominant is his lowest. His top two values are social and utilitarian. Dave will be motivated to help people in useful ways. He also does not like to be pushed to make quick decisions. Dave prefers to be inclusive and get many opinions before he makes decisions. Jennifer has a communication style of a High Influencer. Sam's preference is Dominant. Sam admits that he will need to reign himself in during the conversation and not push the agenda to go faster than is comfortable for Dave. So they agreed to begin the Conversation for Connection this way:

Jennifer: *Dave, thank you for agreeing to meet with us. We know you and your team have done a great deal of work on the performance review policy. Sam and I would like to understand your vision for how the policy works best to help employees and management in useful ways.*

Since their initial purpose of this conversation was for connection with Dave, they spent much of the time listening to his views and asking questions to build understanding. At the end of the meeting, Jennifer moved into a Conversation for Creating New Possibilities by saying, "Dave, I'd like to think more about what you have shared and how we can best work with the policy. After I've given this more thought, I'm wondering if you would be willing to walk through some scenarios with me next week. I am thinking we can have a conversation to explore options and structure and to get input about how you would guide us to stay with the guidelines of the policy while still motivating all the employees. I am open to using my team as a case group so that we can observe the impact of the new policy to see what happens. Are you willing to help me with this?"

This will lead to more conversations. The intention to communicate is clear. Being present in the moment, adapting to change, and knowing which conversation to create next will enable confidence and competence as a communicator to increase.

In another organization, a manager of a large pharmaceutical company, Jean, decided to initiate a conversation about the performance reviews policy with her boss, Jackson. Jean knows her preferred communication style is High Steady and her manager's is High Dominant. She selected the Conversation for Conflict Resolution knowing her boss will appreciate a direct approach even though that is not how she would normally approach a conversation.

Jean began the conversation this way: "I am troubled by having to force rank my employees. I have five team members. All of them have been here for over six years. They are all meeting expectations in their roles. Yet, our policy requires me to rank one of them as "needs improvement." I cannot in good consciousness build a case that one of them is underperforming based on what we have said we want from them. I do not agree with the company policy. I think it is unjust. Jackson, what do you think about this?"

Jean was surprised when Jackson replied, "Jean, I agree with you. I've been battling with Human Resources and my own management about this very issue. Let's put our heads together and figure out what to do to influence them. What action do you think we need to take to get their attention?" An influence strategy that involves meeting with several different stakeholders grows from their conversation. The ability to say it right when it matters most gives us confidence and competence.

In yet another organization, Giada works for a midsized company that has had the same performance policy in place for two years, and she saw firsthand how it impacted her morale and that of her employees. She decided she could not keep her integrity as a manager by continuing to implement this practice. The tipping point for her was when she watched a peer draw a name out of a jar to decide which of his employees would get the "needs improvement" rating this year. When he did it, he said, "All six of my employees bust their butts to perform, and it makes me sick that I have to label one as 'needs improvement.'" Giada believed that it was a losing battle to try to change the policy in the corporation in which she worked. So she had a conversation with herself and decided this was a situation she wanted to disengage from as a way to stand for what she believes in.

Giada began to look for a new position in another company. Her top criterion was to work for an organization that respected individuals and thus that did not manage with a forced performance-ranking management practice. As she began to interview with companies for management positions, she asked questions to learn about their performance management system. She held many Conversations to Create New Possibilities focused on how employees were evaluated. Giada listened very carefully as she spoke with managers in her interviews. She used most of the conversation types during her interviews to ensure she knew what she was getting into.

Giada created a Conversation for Moving On with her former company and a Conversation for Connection with a new one. She decided to take a leadership position with a company that demonstrated it was focused on individual people development without treating people as "resources" or a number. She chose to work for a manager who was respected for leading based on values that she shared. Her manager also had demonstrated that he would take a stand when a Conversation for Conflict Resolution was needed. Giada's experience of work changed when she took a stand for herself and created a better position that aligned with her values.

Final Words

What do you want to influence? What are the conversations you want to create next? Conversations are an opportunity to give and receive a meaningful gift as a result of the exchange. Are you ready to make the change to create more meaning in your communication? Can you say it right when it matters most? When the conversation changes, are you ready for what comes next? When you understand and use emotional intelligence, workplace motivators, preferred communications styles, and each of the 12 types of conversations, you will be a masterful communicator.

You may remember that in Chapter 3, I offered you a complementary assessment to help you get a handle on your own preferred communication style. That invitation still stands.

Special Bonus Offer!

To complete your online assessment, please go to www. The ProfessionalDevelopmentGroup.com and click on the Talent Mastery Assessments button on the left. Then click on the Take Assessments button. Use response link 124439XUB.

Or if you want support in developing your conversation ability, please consider attending the workshop Talent@Work or working with Shawn Kent Hayashi as a coach. In any case, please be sure to visit www.TheProfesionalDevelopmentGroup. com or call 888-959-1188 for additional resources and more information about our workshops and coaching services.

I look forward to having a conversation with you.

Shawn Kent Hayashi

Index

About the Author

Shawn Kent Hayashi is the founder of The Professional Development Group and author of five business communication books. Using an assessment-based approach, her company helps people improve their emotional intelligence and communication skills, build stronger relationships and teams, and make more effective presentations. She also helps clients apply the assessment methodology in their own organizations. Clients include Fortune 500 and mid-sized companies, universities, and entrepreneurial organizations. An Emotional Intelligence Certified Coach, Hayashi earned an M.S. in organization dynamics from the University of Pennsylvania and holds many certifications in assessment analysis. She also serves on the boards of several professional organizations including the advisory board of the University of Pennsylvania's Masters in Organization Dynamics and the board of the Philadelphia Human Resources Planning Society. In addition, she is active in the Forum of Executive Women. Shawn lives in Lansdale, Pennsylvania, with her husband and son.

Shawn Kent Hayashi can be reached at The Professional Development Group, 888-959-1188, or at info@TheProfessionalDevelopmentGroup.com.

Book Shawn to Speak

For conferences or corporate events, Shawn's presentations get people engaged and participating! She uses assessments so each attendee gets a clear picture of his or her preferred communication style, workplace motivators, and emotional intelligence. She will tailor her presentation to your conference theme and event.

Shawn Kent Hayashi's keynote package includes:

Premeeting prep
Meaningful keynote
Breakfast or lunch with Shawn for your sponsors or board
Breakout sessions for participants to practice what they
    learned

Call 888-959-1188 or visit www.TheProfessionalDevelopment Group.com or www.ShawnKent.com to book Shawn today!

Special Bonus Offer!

To complete your online assessment, please go to www.The ProfessionalDevelopmentGroup.com, and click on the Talent Mastery Assessments button on the left. Then click on the Take Assessments button. Use response link 124439XUB.